What people are say

The True Origins or jesus

The True Origins of Jesus by Geoff Roberts, will save you years of research by giving the answers your inquiring mind is thirsting for. It bridges the gap between truth and myth, with a common sense that is difficult to find these days in discourses about Jesus.

Dean Wilkinson, Founder of Epochwork.com

What caught my attention about Geoff's book is his honest and open desire to explore the origins of Christianity from an unbiased historical perspective, and his non - theological approach is refreshing and illuminating.

Colm Holland, author of *The Secret of The Alchemist*

'The True Origins of Jesus' is an important and timely book. It disrupts, challenges and invites you to look at the teachings of the Bible through a more enlightened, unbiased and informed lens.

Geoff Roberts' direct, humble, articulate voice speaks softly but with great power to present a well researched and informed account of Jesus the man, not Jesus the myth. Be prepared to accept that your understanding of who you thought Jesus was may be entirely wrong.

The layers of false teachings are exposed with an elegance and compassion that only those touched by a more divine hand can do.

Geoff Roberts is no false prophet. He speaks a truth that many will not want to hear but one that we all (especially at these times of turmoil, falsehood and fake news) desperately need to hear.

This book may bring you to the end of a road that you have been travelling. It will also set you on a path that will liberate, inform and help you understand, in this lifetime, the power of love that connects us all. Always has. Always will.

The truth about the origins of Jesus really will, as Jesus (probably) said, 'set you free'.

Roy Leighton Co-author of 'A Moon on Water - activities and stories for developing Children's Spiritual Intelligence' and Co-chair of the 'Cambridge Peace and Education Research Group' (CPERG)

Through the ages, religious faith and historical fact have enjoyed a slippery relationship. Taboo and group-think make it hard for those who wish to question entrenched beliefs. In "The True Origins of Jesus" Geoff Roberts brilliantly clears away the fog. With clarity and courage, he walks us through the origins of the Jesus stories and the various sources of the New Testament writings. Unafraid to set the original Jesus stories in their proper setting among contemporary bodies of philosophical literature, Geoff reveals some truly arresting correlations, with far-reaching implications for how we understand the figure of Jesus and the Biblical literature which surrounds him. Whether you begin with a perspective of faith or non-faith, you will certainly enjoy sharing Geoff Roberts' scholarly and open exploration. And I guarantee you will come away stimulated and challenged.

Paul Wallis
Author of *Escaping from Eden, The Scars of Eden* and *Echoes of Eden*

The True Origins
of Jesus

The True Origins of Jesus

Geoff Roberts

Edited by

Colm Holland

CHRISTIAN ALTERNATIVE
BOOKS

Winchester, UK
Washington, USA

JOHN HUNT PUBLISHING

First published by Christian Alternative Books, 2022
Christian Alternative Books is an imprint of John Hunt Publishing Ltd.,
No. 3 East St., Alresford, Hampshire SO24 9EE, UK
office@jhpbooks.com
www.johnhuntpublishing.com
www.christian-alternative.com

For distributor details and how to order please visit the 'Ordering' section on our website.

Text copyright: Geoff Roberts 2021

ISBN: 978 1 78904 904 6
978 1 78904 905 3 (ebook)
Library of Congress Control Number: 2021945737

Edited by Colm Holland

A CIP catalogue record for this book is available from the British Library.

Design: Matthew Greenfield

UK: Printed and bound by CPI Group (UK) Ltd, Croydon, CR0 4YY
Printed in North America by CPI GPS partners

We operate a distinctive and ethical publishing philosophy in all areas of our business, from our global network of authors to production and worldwide distribution.

Contents

Foreword by Dean Wilkinson

The truth shall set you free. Jesus of Nazareth

The True Origins of Jesus by Geoff Roberts, will save you years of research by giving the answers your inquiring mind is thirsting for. It bridges the gap between truth and myth, with a common sense that is difficult to find these days in discourses about Jesus.

An internet search that includes such terms as: origins of the Bible, God, Christian, Christ, and especially Jesus, most often results in frustration for the average researcher wading through the bias lying within the contents of their findings.

Finding unbiased books is just as hard. However, in this book, Geoff Roberts has assembled unbiased factual information about the history of Jesus of Nazareth that feels like a peaceful oasis in the desert and leaves clues for those of us whose thirst is insatiable. If only I had discovered this information earlier, I could have shaved years off my own search.

I still recall what it felt like entering that wilderness of information. I was outside with my laptop on a beautiful summer afternoon in Michigan, camping on the St. Clair river looking across the border into Canada with nowhere to go and nothing else to do. Suddenly, I stumbled upon the internet trailhead I was looking for about the origins of the Bible. As I read the material available, the thrill of new "truths", as well as the dread of possibly being wrong about everything I believed in, was overwhelming. I gently shut my laptop to let what I had just discovered settle into my new reality.

I had been suspecting some "trickery" in the orthodox Church teaching based on what I had been seeing during my more than twenty years in Christian leadership. It had been seven years since I had resigned from my last position and I

1

had delayed any earnest effort to confirm my suspicions before now, because of what it would mean if they were correct. After leaving the Church, the material I consumed expanded across religions, philosophies, histories, and the most recent scientific discoveries.

One by one layers of falsehood and fears were shed like a snake sheds its skin as I compared fact with myth. That sunny summer day I sat staring across the border between the two countries, I was feeling like a refugee far from home wanting to get back to what was safe and familiar. For a few days, I wanted to return home, my former beliefs intact and my mind blissfully ignorant. A quest for the historical truth should, before it starts, be carefully considered against the bliss of naivete. I had to screw up the courage to continue my quest believing that the truth would set me free.

I hope you have come upon this book because you are seeking the truth that will set you free. I know that this book prevents years of painstaking research, hoping for a scrap of truth amidst the desert of information available to us today.

Be prepared to open your mind and face the reality of never being able to go back to naivete. There is more information about the true origins of Jesus packed in this book than most people will find in a lifetime of searching. Proceed courageously and humbly as you discover these truths that can not only set you free, but also test your resolve! You will be glad you did.

What, you may ask, may happen to your current beliefs? In my experience, you will mourn the loss of your childish beliefs. You may even get angry. You may feel guilty and gullible. You may get a little frightened just as I did. I also suggest, you will be better for it. It's not like you will no longer have anything to believe in. It is just the first step in a new direction, a new way of believing in something bigger than ourselves. There will still be room for faith; a new kind of faith. There will be love, in fact, the capacity to love expands. There is still hope that this life is not all there is. Faith, hope, and love will always be true, always human, always accessible, always believable. Always beautiful.

So, let yourself revoke the stories that have held you captive and you will have the space to embrace those that set you free. Courageously deconstruct the house you have built upon sand. Humbly re-imagine how you might restructure a new home on a firmer foundation. A faith that can withstand any storm life throws at you while also empowering some peace of mind. Peace is the state humans flourish in.

One look around at the chaos in the world today certainly reveals we can use a little less strife and discord on our planet and in our own lives. Set that intention as you read this book and have faith all is well; hope the truth will set you free and be sure to forgive yourself and any others for the lies we have all believed. Let any and all the emotions you feel roll through you and allow yourself to feel the love for truth that filled Geoff as he dedicated himself to researching and writing this book.

Rest here, it is an oasis in the desert. Truth often shocks the system, but it also frees the soul.

Isn't that what your quest in life has been so far? If you have picked up a book like this, it says something about you. You are probably in pursuit of growth, not just knowledge. You crave some peace of mind, some rest for your soul. You are not alone in that pursuit. As one who has been on this journey, let my promise to you be: if knowledge about the roots of Christianity is what you are seeking, you will surely find it.

The most real thing about us humans is that we are all in pursuit of something more. It is also true that in our hunger we are often led off course along the way. It is hard not to be. Everyone and everything promise to trade their idea of what will make us happy for some of our time or money. We pursue wealth, possessions, fame, knowledge, and power because it promises to feel good. And it does. For a minute. That feeling fails to create a prosperous reality inside or out. I believe there is a reason we are designed to pursue, to grow, to evolve. The expansion of love is what we truly seek. Love cannot be observed scientifically or known logically. It is experienced at a soul level. Love is the only thing that seems to quench our thirst, to feed our souls' hunger for more.

Maybe that is why humans have always been expert mythmakers and amateur sense makers. Myth captures what our hearts and souls long for. A glimpse of the eternal, a promise that our lives mean something beyond the few years we have on this planet. The tragedy and the comedy, the drama and mystery of life are best captured in the stories we tell. We seem to be hardwired to make sense of our lives through myth. Starting from our Neanderthal roots, we have always sought to understand life and death, and to give meaning to the magic of our world. On walls of rock, leaves of plants, papyrus scrolls, paper, and now computer screens, pictures and symbols are all pointing skyward, as we keep trying to communicate what feels like we need to be true.

We will probably never capture the totality of this mystery with symbols, science or myth. Maybe it is hidden for our benefit. If we somehow made perfect sense of it, we would stop trying, stop searching. It is in the pursuit that we grow and evolve into what is wrapped solidly in myths of our making.

Can we embrace the myths and still make sense of Christ?

If you have been on this journey for long, maybe you have discovered that Jesus and Christ are not one and the same. In the stories we have of Jesus, he did not claim the name of Christ. That surname was written into the story later, for the initial followers to make sense of, and to connect the dots in their minds. That is also where all the trouble began. Before that time, the world accepted the mystery of a divine Creator and left alone the need to dissect and connect the spiritual to the rational.

As Richard Rohr states in *The Universal Christ: How a Forgotten*

Reality Can Change Everything We See, Hope for and Believe, SPCK Publishing, 2019, "the notion of faith that emerged in the West was much more a rational assent to the truth of certain mental beliefs, rather than a calm and hopeful truth that God is inherent in all things, and that this whole thing is going somewhere good."

Rohr also points out that the Jesus story does not have him claiming he was any more divine than anyone else. Instead, he seemed to be "describing the 'Way' by which all humans and religions must allow matter and Spirit to operate as one."

Christ is easier to understand when we separate the idea from the name Jesus. The idea of Christ is that the wholeness of creation since the beginning of time and until the end is all "One Thing". We have encoded in our DNA the spiritual mystery of a creator we have never been separate from except in our rational minds. We can feel separate, but we can't *be* separate. That is one of the most exciting ideas we are experiencing as a species today. We are all a collective consciousness of individuals making up the whole.

Carl Jung termed this the "whole making instinct", the God archetype in every one of us. We are all in this together, whatever, and wherever this is. I believe we can embrace the mystery and the truth that there is something in all of us longing for something we have no perfect language for. Christ seems as good as any other. God, Source, Energy, Nature, Light, Love, Brahmā and Jesus work just fine too. "Jesus can hold together one group or religion, Christ can hold together everything," said Richard Rohr.

The spiritual non-religious have exploded in numbers in the last couple of decades. Christians have been engaged in a silent exodus of biblical proportions from the Church. Finding that the Church, religion, and professionals trained to explain the mystery have no satisfying answers for the questions they have, millions have been leaving every year. It seems myths do not hold up well under scientific or factual inquiry in the age of the internet. If Christianity had not insisted on rational concepts such as inerrancy of the Bible, doctrine, dogma, and formal statements of belief to "be saved" from hell, it is possible it could survive. After all, it is a good idea. A place people can go to be with others, a day set aside to contemplate the mystery and unity of life.

Geoff's work supports my own understanding, as it cries out for a new kind of "Christianity". One that embraces all people and all things as divine – god like, beautiful and powerful. A collective working towards one thing in unity and in unison. Most likely it would have to change its name. Christ may never be able to separate from Jesus in our collective consciousness. In 2000 years, it may be different, but for now we would do well as a species to embrace our oneness and then live like it is true. We can call it whatever works for us. Perhaps for a while we can just all agree to call it Love.

I believe God does not care what we call it or name it in our feeble attempts to describe it. It is everywhere and in everything and seems to have no preference.

This book will not suggest the end of faith, spirituality, or our pursuit of understanding. It does suggest that as an evolving species it may serve us to build a faith that works in life and for life.

As we get to know ourselves, become more self-aware, and empathetic in our nature, it will serve our conscience and the collective wellbeing to stop insisting on a singular identity for our heroes. What if we could only tell stories about Batman, Superman, Thor, and Wonder Woman – then Zeus would not exist? We make up names to tell good stories, to hold the narrative together, but insisting there is only one story is too much to ask of our mythmaking natures. Perhaps we can make sense of them in another life. In this life we are free to choose and believe what we want if it works for us. As Paul is quoted in

Galatians, "It is for freedom that Christ set us free."

With freedom comes responsibility. There are two kinds of freedom: freedom from and freedom to. Freedom *from*, implies you are, or were, a captive; a victim of something or someone. Freedom *to* – empowers you to bigger and better possibilities; to *more*.

Freedom *to* – will lead to discovering the reality of joy, peace, and the abundance of Love we have within our hearts. That kind of freedom can also lead you to a new kind of faith; one that expands our human capabilities and understanding. We live in exciting times. Humanity is evolving at an unprecedented speed. Isn't it time our ideas of God evolve too?

It is my sincere hope that *The True Origins of Jesus* will assist our individual roles in this evolution.

Dean Wilkinson, Founder of Epochwork.com, Illinois, USA, 2021.

Editorial Note

The late Geoff Roberts originally self-published this book under the title *Jesus 888* in 2012, and it is now out of print. It came to my attention through Niels Jorgen Lindtner, who recently translated and published this work in Danish. Niels' father, the late Dr Christian Lindtner, is cited within the text in Geoff's book as the authority on ancient Sanskrit texts and the origins of Buddhism. I had the privilege of knowing Christian and admire his ground-breaking work.

What caught my attention about Geoff's book was his honest and open desire to explore the origins of Christianity from an unbiased historical perspective, and his non-theological approach is refreshing and illuminating. Geoff was an intelligent, non-academic who wanted to conduct his own research into the evidence available to all of us, regarding the origins of the "greatest story ever told" and to ask the question of whether it can be supported by any historical evidence outside of the pages of the Bible.

The results of Geoff's investigation are extensive, conclusive, and approachable for anyone with an open mind and even a small degree of intellectual curiosity. As Geoff discovers in this book and George Gershwin wrote in his musical *Porgy and Bess*, "The things that you're liable, to read in the Bible, it ain't necessarily so."

I have made some minor edits to Geoff's original work with the permission of his family; in part so that the highly credible source material he used can be more readily referred to by anyone who wants to read further.

I am also conscious that at this time of writing, new discoveries of *The Dead Sea Scrolls* may reveal even more historical evidence to support Geoff's findings.

My own understanding of the origins of Christianity has

been greatly improved by Geoff's tireless work and my thanks go to John Hunt Publishing for enabling this important book to reach a larger and broader audience.

Colm Holland, author of *The Secret of The Alchemist*, O-books, 2020.

Glastonbury, England, 2021.

Acknowledgements

This small book, designed to stimulate your thinking about the literal biblical "truths", which are for many of us set in stone, would not have been possible without the huge support and motivation provided by the two most important women in my life, my wife, Audrey, and daughter, Kristen.

Special thanks too, to my good friends John and Norman, both of whom spent many hours discussing with me the subjects which have appeared in the pages that follow and especially, my thoughts regarding gematria.

John, who would berate me mercilessly, when it became too profound and Norman, who analysed every argument, were both enormously supportive.

And finally, a special thanks to Tom and Elaine, who provided endless tea and toast at their cafe, The Auberge, in Liverpool, England, where much of the research into some very heavy tomes, was carried out.

Geoff Roberts, Liverpool, England. 2012.

Before the gospels were adopted as history, no record exists that Jesus was ever in the city of Jerusalem at all; or anywhere else on earth.

Earl Doherty: *The Jesus Puzzle: Did Christianity Begin with a Mythical Christ?* Age of Reason Publications, 2005.

Introduction

The life and times of the Christian Saviour, Jesus Christ, have influenced the development of the western world for nearly two thousand years, not only providing spiritual sustenance for millions of believers but also a source of many a good plot in films and novels, over the past century.

It truly is the greatest story ever told and maybe that is all it is: a story!

Like most people, the sum of my knowledge about the origins of the Christian Messiah and indeed the whole Christian concept, was what I had gleaned from my religious education lessons at school. On reflection, it was not very much.

The story, as far as I could see, was one of a miraculous birth to a virgin, who having a problem with overnight accommodation, gave birth in a stable to a Jewish Saviour, fathered by the Jewish God, Yahweh.

The baby grew into a miracle worker, healing the sick and raising the dead, followed by a group of local fishermen and eventually paid the ultimate price for upsetting the Jewish priests and thus became the Saviour of the world.

If that sounds all a bit simplistic, at the time that I was at school, it was. I never delved any deeper into the story. I finished my schooling believing that the story that had passed through time was a true reflection of the happenings at the time and there was no doubt about this, because everybody else believed it. Didn't they?

As I matured, I developed a passionate interest in the history of ancient cultures and the religions of the Egyptians, Greeks, Romans and all those peoples involved in the early civilizations that were being created as far back as four thousand years ago and more.

It dawned on me, quite early in my explorations, that there

was a mine of information available, both from archaeological sources and ancient texts, about the Mediterranean cults that were being followed and how these beliefs had originated using a system of complicated philosophy, astronomy, and math, which had produced the societies of ancient Egypt and Greece and their associated superhero gods.

These people, looked upon in modern times as pagans, most certainly did not conform to how we commonly view pagans.

They were not simple country folk who painted their bodies blue in war and lacked any education. They were the creators of some of the finest examples of architecture, such as the Parthenon and wrote wonderful prose, such as Homer's *Iliad* and *Odyssey*.

The history of their societies was fascinating and enlightening and stimulated my desire to investigate the early beginnings of the Christians and their superhero, Jesus Christ the Messiah.

School had left me with the impression that everything in the Bible was historically correct, leaving no need to look elsewhere for confirmation.

By now, armed with a knowledge of the ancients and their incredible achievements, I knew that there just had to be more to the Christian story and how it came about and there was probably so much more to know, too, about its foundation stone, the Lord Jesus Christ.

Little did I know then, just how much more there was to know. I began an investigative journey of what became almost an obsession and I was stunned by some of the findings.

My investigation took me through many diverse avenues including ancient Egypt, ancient Greece, Persia, all over the Holy Land and most tellingly and astonishingly, into the pages of books relating to mathematics and what we know as Sacred Geometry.

Using only factual information that was available, and there was lots of it, the results have changed my perception of one of our best-known religions forever.

It is not my intention to offend or otherwise upset those

for whom their faith in a literal interpretation of the Bible is paramount, but in my experience of this investigation, faith and scholarship do not make for good bedfellows.

They do not always sit comfortably side by side and sometimes the results of research can be hard to stomach.

The findings have pointed me in a direction, which for most people, even those with only a passing interest in the story, will find to be earth shattering.

An almost infinite number of books have been written on the subject of the historical Jesus; many have been written by learned academics for similar academics and this is why most of the remarkable facts about the supposed Jesus, have never reached the general population.

In compiling this body of evidence, I hope to be able to bring those very facts into the public arena in a readable and hopefully, easy to understand language that will bring to light important elements of the origins of the Christian faith, known by a privileged few and enhance the understanding for everybody.

Some people will simply refuse to confront the problems of a literal interpretation of the Bible that I will unearth, and I suppose, this will always be the case.

Faith alone cannot explain some of the very difficult questions that I will come up against and the fact that a statement is made in the Bible does not confirm the historical accuracy of that statement. History needs independent sources and a deeper investigation into the roots of the subject I am examining.

I will step outside of the pages of the New Testament and try to establish where and why the stories were originally fabricated and most importantly, how the religions of the non-Christian people at the start of the first century CE, may have influenced the thinking of the gospel writers.

I will examine how those old religions influenced the early Jewish Christians and I will look at books, texts and gospels, such as the Gnostic gospels, little known outside the corridors of academia. It is truly amazing how many Christian apologists, people who can quote the Bible at will, have no knowledge at all of one of the most significant historical finds of the twentieth century, the Gnostic gospels.

I cannot stress too often, how much more information is available relating to any one of the subjects that we discuss in this short analysis of the Christian origins. My intention is simply to introduce you to a world of religions and philosophies that many people are totally unaware of. Without this background knowledge, it is impossible to understand the highly complicated foundations of the Christian story and indeed, the many diverse groups, all known as Christians, who saw this story in so many ways.

My conversations with most orthodox Christians, and that includes senior Church ministers, have left me feeling very frustrated. Very few have been willing to even listen to some of the more complicated elements of my quest and virtually none of them are aware of the significance of the massively important subject of Gematria, which is very much in evidence in the Old and New Testaments, and as I frequently point out, many people think that if they do not know about a particular subject, then it does not actually exist.

My investigation took me to a world of shapes and numbers involving geniuses like Pythagoras, Plato and unknown astronomers who knew their way around the cosmos and left the evidence for us to examine.

So, with all the evidence compiled here, including some which has only come to light relatively recently, you too can draw your own conclusions from a story which will look very different to the one you learned at school.

It is now my belief that Jesus Christ was a mythical figure and was never intended by the early founders of the religion, to be a walking, talking historical person.

For them, he was a spirit; but let me start at the beginning.

Chapter 1

The Quest Begins

If you ask any committed Christian what evidence they perceive as a firm foundation for a truly historical Jesus figure that walked the Holy Land, performing miracles and creating the origins of a remarkable world religion, they will quote the pages of the Old and New Testaments as their only source material.

The words of Paul and the highly educated scholars who composed the gospels of Mark, Matthew, Luke and John, sound very convincing and one would assume that this was about the sum total of available Christian writing which has passed down to us in the form of the Holy Bible and as such, is an authentic account of the birth, life and death of the Saviour worshipped by so many.

Historians and theologians know this is very far from the truth. Apart from the historical texts known to the orthodox Christian and indeed, the non-Christian, there are a huge number of other ancient writings, which reflect on the early days of the fledgling faith.

Little is spoken by the modern Church about these early writings as they do not always support the Christian message as the Church would like to see it.

If I am to achieve anything in my investigation into the reality behind the Christian origins and the validity of a historical, walking, talking, living Jesus, we must examine all the ingredients in the extremely complicated equation and in a totally realistic way and abandon the idea that faith alone will prove a point one way or the other.

One such ingredient that screams out for further attention is the existence of other scriptures, known as the Gnostic gospels. I must start my quest with a knowledge of these little-known gospels because they take us into another world of ancient thinking that is absolutely essential to understand if the reader is to grasp the profound philosophy that ultimately gave rise to the foundations of Christianity as we know it today.

The word Gnostic comes from the Greek word gnosis, meaning knowledge in the sense of enlightenment and as such, the gospels were composed by people with a very different slant on the Christian story.

Heavy tomes have been written about these ancient texts and in my opinion, none better than *The Gnostic Gospels*, by Professor Elaine Pagels from Princeton University, W&N, 2006; an easy to read, in depth study.

What are they and where did they come from? Who wrote them and why? These questions are often asked when the subject of the gospels arises.

Historians for a long time knew of the existence of the alternative gospels, now classified under the title of New Testament Apocrypha, as fragments had been found in various archaeological excavations but frustratingly, they had little to work on to establish any real historical significance.

Ironically, too, scholars knew of their early existence by the criticisms heaped upon them by the Church father Irenaeus, who realized the danger they posed to the orthodox faith. Around the year 180 CE, as the Bishop of Lyons, he produced his well-known work, *Against the Heresies* or *Adversus Haereses*, which was a detailed attack on the whole concept of the Gnostic belief.

Before discussing these works in some depth, it is worth looking at where and how they were found.

In the winter of 1945, a peasant boy, Muhammad Ali Al Samman and his two brothers, were working in the area around the town of Nag Hammadi in Upper Egypt when, while digging for fertilizer, they unearthed a large clay jar which they broke apart, hoping to find gold and treasure.

Little did they realize that they had made a find, which would turn the accepted story of Jesus Christ on its head.

The pot contained a cache of papyrus books, thirteen in all and in the now well-known story, he and his brothers took their find home, where their mother used some of the texts as fuel for the fire!

From here the story takes on something of the theme from an Indiana Jones movie, as the value of the codices (papyrus books) were recognized by a local historian, who had them examined in Cairo, where they were sold on the black market. Most of the codices ended up with the Egyptian government who deposited them in the Coptic Museum in Cairo.

One of the books found its way to the United States and was offered for sale, where ultimately it came to the attention of the highly respected historian Gilles Quispel who, having acquired it, realized that he had in his possession the whole text of the Gospel of Thomas. A text described as a secret gospel containing many of the sayings of Jesus Christ but in a context unfamiliar to readers of the New Testament.

It was not long before the fifty-two texts from Nag Hammadi, including the Gospel of Philip, the Gospel of Truth and the Apocalypse of Peter, took on a life of their own and could no longer be ignored by the Church, who would have to recognize the revolutionary nature of their contents.

The texts from the earthenware jar were written in Coptic and were dated by scholars to around the years of 350 CE to 400 CE, much later than the New Testament gospels, but were translations of the original Greek, written at a much earlier date of maybe 130 CE.

The religious scholar Professor Helmut Koester of Harvard University has suggested that some elements of the Gospel of Thomas may have been created as early as the second part of the first century and possibly even predating the Synoptic gospels and the *Gospel of John* in the New Testament, written according to most scholars circa 70 CE to 140 CE.

It should be noted, however, that gospel dating has never been an accurate science and a decade's inaccuracy and even more, would not be surprising.

The writers of these gospels were early Christians who perceived the whole concept of the Jesus story in a completely different light to those who accepted the gospels of Mark, Matthew, Luke and John as the only true reflection of the holy story.

As a result, the bishops of the rapidly strengthening orthodox Church, or those with a literalist view of the New Testament gospels, viewed the Gnostics as heretics of the worst kind.

It was easy to understand why, when you consider that these alternative texts, coming from various groups who also followed the teachings of Jesus, would deny the reality of the virgin birth and even the bodily resurrection of Christ himself.

The Gnostics were an obvious threat to the Church in the second century CE and as such had to be suppressed, a job they did well so that little or nothing was known of the various alternative sects, until the spectacular find at Nag Hammadi.

Even worse, as far as the bishops were concerned, the Gnostic faith had no time for bishops, priests or any hierarchy. This was a major issue for those who would use the idea of apostolic succession as a way of maintaining their own hold on power.

And hold on they did. Early Church Fathers from the second century CE onwards, spent much time and effort in composing vast volumes criticizing their opponents for their blasphemies.

Irenaeus produced a series of books called, *The Destruction and Overthrow of Falsely So Called Knowledge,* in which he tried to demonstrate the absurdity and inconsistency of the works of the heretics.

Before we dig deeper into the works and history of the Gnostics, it would be interesting to note that the name was not used at the time to describe these other Christian sects.

The name Gnostic was used much later to distinguish them from the orthodox groups. They were simply Christians but of a different viewpoint.

Trying to establish the earliest origins of the Gnostic movement is almost impossible and scholars have argued their foundation for many years.

There is undoubtedly a strong influence within the gospels that points to Hellenistic philosophy with Platonic elements very evident. Equally, it can be argued that there is a very strong probability that the texts were influenced by Eastern mysticism, more of which I will discuss in a later chapter.

The Hellenised Jews who developed the Gnostic Christian stories, were different in just about every way to how they perceived Jesus and their God figure, as opposed to the Orthodox believers who maintained the veracity of their belief in the authentic gospels.

Even the very basics of the creation story demonstrated a major difference and an insoluble one at that.

The Gnostics viewed Yahweh, the God of the Old Testament and the God of Israel as a subordinate being to the real God, who lived in another realm of existence.

The lesser god, known as the Demiurge, from Plato's dialogue *Timaeus*, was much inferior and was responsible for the world's ills and whose intention was to keep mankind immersed in ignorance and would punish those who searched for the truth.

The Gnostic teaching explained a doctrine that all material reality is evil and the *raison d'être* of their religion was to identify with the divine spark trapped within ourselves and the achievement of Gnosis through teaching and following a path of complicated philosophy, releasing that spark or seed from the matter in which it was trapped.

The real God had given rise to entities known as Aeons, which lived in a celestial ether or realm of light called the Pleroma or the Fullness of God.

It was one of these divine entities, Sophia, the female manifestation of God's wisdom, which gave rise to Yaldabaoth or Yahweh of the Old Testament.

This creator God gave rise to Adam and Eve but with the seed of the divine trapped within them and it was through the teachings of the spiritual Jesus that the mysteries of the kingdom could be unlocked, and the initiate would ultimately find the oneness with the true God in the realm of the Pleroma. Having achieved this, the Gnostic had found the Christ within himself.

It is self-evident that the Gnostics pursued a highly spiritual form of their Christianity and maintained a belief that the gospels of the New Testament were only an introduction to the real meaning of the divine message.

They categorized people into three distinct groups. The lower group known as the Hylics were those considered beyond salvation. They lacked spirit and cared only for matters of the flesh and were not capable of the spiritual journey required for Gnosis.

The Psychics were a sort of middle group, who might attain a lesser salvation through faith and teaching, whereas the Pneumatics were highly spiritually aware and could be considered amongst the highest order of humans and were able to escape the doom of the material world by acquiring the secret knowledge or Gnosis.

The Gnostic sects of the second and third centuries CE were certainly not a homogenous group, sharing similar spiritual beliefs and philosophies.

Their view of the nature of Jesus as the Christ differed, depending upon which group you study.

There were those who considered Jesus as a redeeming, liberating spirit. A revealer who was sent by the Supreme God of Truth to rescue mankind from the influence of the evil Demiurge (public craftsman in Greek) and allow the individual to return to the spiritual home, the Pleroma, at his death. As such, Jesus was perceived as purely spirit, a concept known as docetism, where Christ inhabited a phantom body and only appeared to be human. They could not conceive the idea that a Holy Messenger sent from the true God could suffer and die in the manner of a mere mortal, thus seeing the resurrection in a purely spiritual way. They did not believe in the physical resurrection of the flesh.

On the other hand, there were groups who saw Jesus Christ as human, born naturally of earthly parents but at the time of baptism, the dove of God conferred the divine spark in him and he became the teacher or emissary from the One.

At the time of his death, that spirit departed the now dead body and resurrected, rejoining the father in the Realm of Light.

"Yes, they saw me, they punished me. It was another, their father, who drank the gall and the vinegar, it was not I. They struck me with the reed; it was another, Simon, who bore the cross on his shoulder. I was another upon whom they placed the crown of thorns. But I was rejoicing in the height over all the wealth of the Archons [lower order of material creators] and the offspring of their error, of their empty glory. I was laughing at their ignorance"(From the *Second Treatise of the Great Seth*, Nag Hammadi Library).

Time and time again, the Gnostic version of divine teaching was shown to be at odds with the ideas of the developing orthodox Christian Church with its bishops and priests determined to wipe out the threat to their authority.

Even the most basic concept of the creation story, that of Adam and Eve in the Garden of Eden, was turned on its head in the text of the *Testimony of Truth* (Nag Hammadi Library), where the story is told from the serpent's point of view who, representing to the Gnostics, a divine wisdom, tries to persuade mankind to expand its knowledge. The false God of the Old Testament is not happy with this and threatens all sorts of repercussions.

As Elaine Pagels points out in her book *The Gnostic Gospels*, the view of the orthodox Christian and Jew, was one of total separation from humanity and God. God was a totally separate entity but some of the Gnostics who wrote their gospels believed that achieving that knowledge of the divine spark within, was to achieve self-knowledge and self-knowledge was knowledge of God. As Pagels explains, "The self and the divine are identical."

Markedly, the gnostic Jesus seems more inclined to want to teach a pathway of enlightenment than to discuss the sins of man and demonstrates himself as a guide to this ultimate aim and having achieved it, the initiate becomes the equal of the Master.

Similarly, Jesus tells Thomas that as they have both received their origins from the same source, upon achieving Gnosis, they will become equals.

"I am not your master. Because you have drunk, you have become drunk from the bubbling stream, which I have measured out. He who will drink from my mouth will become as I am. I myself shall become he, and the things that are hidden will be revealed to him" (Gospel of Thomas, Nag Hammadi Library).

It cannot be expressed too often how words like, "and the things that are hidden will be revealed to him", are another example of the secret nature of the true meanings, not only within the Gnostic gospels but within the stories of the New Testament itself.

It is a hard concept to grasp, for a regular, church going orthodox Christian to have to change their whole view of what the gospels are saying. As George Gershwin astutely declared, when he included these memorable words in a song: "The things that you're liable, to read in the Bible, it ain't necessarily so." How true that turned out to be.

The Gnostics and the composers of the New Testament were masters of the written word of their day, but it was at a very different time to what we know and understand today. They were written in allegory and myth with, no doubt, some factual historical detail included as well.

Myth and allegory were not new to them. They understood

the background to the stories based on mythological detail going back centuries before their time. Concealed within, were the hidden meanings, which the reader, through a teaching, which gave the deeper understanding, could take on board the spiritual message for what it was.

Jesus frequently talks about the mysteries of the kingdom, both in the Gnostic and New Testament gospels, which is how the gospel writers indicated to the early readers that there was a lot more going on here than a story that could be understood by the lowly and the uneducated.

We will probably never know who actually authored any of the Gnostic gospels or indeed those supposedly written by Mark, Matthew, Luke and John.

In those ancient times, writing under the assumed name of an apostle was considered an act of homage. Pseudepigrapha, as it is known, was viewed very differently and not as forgery as it would today.

What they all had in common, was that a story had to be understood on several levels and what the Gnostics believed, was that Jesus was the teacher who could lead the way along the path of Gnosis, resulting in the spiritual realization of what the holy story was really about.

The Synoptic gospels of Mark, Matthew and Luke and indeed the Gospel of John and certainly Revelation, do certainly contain hidden secrets of the kingdom within their verses and in a very interesting, even astounding way. More of this element in the *Divine Equation* in a later chapter.

It was my own personal discovery of the Gnostic gospels that turned my attention, over many years now, to the search for the historical Jesus, if indeed there ever was an historical Jesus.

I was stunned to learn that the early days of the Christian Church were a time of numerous diverse faiths, where groups of Jesus followers, depending on which Gnostic master they studied, could have such a different belief about something which I thought was as simple as the potted history passed down to us via the Gospel of Mark.

For as diverse as the Christian faith is in its present day, including all those differences of faith involved in Catholicism and the multiple Protestant and Orthodox Churches, they are still more united in their basic beliefs than they were all those centuries ago.

The various churches of the current time still maintain a belief in the only true gospels of Mark, Matthew, Luke and John. They maintain the Apostles' Creed and they adhere to the basic institutional structure of the Church.

These essential principles only became established in the late second century and we know from Irenaeus that at his time and before his time, the followers of Jesus, later to be called Christians, were reading texts that would eventually disappear, almost completely, from the orthodox Christian landscape. It dawned on me that some serious politics were at work here and the Church of the late second century CE had worked hard to remove from history, all those spiritually aware groups of Christ followers, who were heavily influenced by the profound thinking of Hellenistic philosophical teachings.

It became obvious to me that the traditions of the various Gnostic sects, their beliefs, their Gnostic leaders, had all been superbly written out of history by the Catholic Church, as time went on.

I, like so many others, had no knowledge at all of these lost gospels and how many have been lost completely, never to be seen again?

When I learned more about the Nag Hammadi find, I was determined to learn as much as I could about the rest of the story which had been so cleverly hidden from me and anybody else interested in Christian origins, for so long.

At the beginning of the third century the cleansing job was well under way and by the time Constantine gave his support to the orthodox faith, the Gnostics were well and truly doomed.

The Nag Hammadi find has, in some quarters, rekindled many of those old problems and the Church has to accept that there are other versions of their gospel, which to the people of their day, had as much meaning to them as the New Testament gospels did for all those throughout the later millennia.

Readers who will be inclined to read more about the early Gnostic traditions will find volumes of highly informative works relating to the subject and throughout their pages, names of the Gnostic fathers will appear with some regularity. Names like Simon Magus, Basilides, Valentinus, Marcion, Cerinthus, Carpocrates, Theudas and Mani, all gave rise to Gnostic schools which separated out into different belief structures.

It would be opportune now to look a little closer at some of these founders if we are to have a deeper understanding of what they stood for.

Not only will we look at the founders, but we should look a little more into the gospels themselves and see just how much they differ from normal Bible teaching, which so inflamed the passions of Irenaeus and other founders of the early church.

Chapter 2

The Gnostic Godfathers

When discussing Gnostic teachers, it must be remembered that the philosophy we now know as Gnosticism actually predates the time of the Christian story by several centuries, as it is a system of personal enlightenment, which was a personal search for the divine within and could be applied to other beliefs apart from Christianity.

With that in mind, the early Church saw a character called Simon Magus, as probably the first of the Gnostic fathers in a pseudo-Christian sense.

What little we know of him comes, as usual, mainly from his detractors and the stories about him were probably composed to shed as much criticism on him as they could, with the boundaries of truth and fiction hard to discern.

Irenaeus, that tireless campaigner for orthodoxy, labelled him "the father of all heretics" and was backed up in his condemnations by Justin Martyr (100–165 CE),who wrote about Simon about a hundred years after his supposed death.

Simon was known as Simon the Sorcerer and Simon of Gitta and was a Samaritan and is considered as the founder of the Gnostic sect called the Simonians. He is actually mentioned in the New Testament in Acts 8:9–24.

"But there was a certain man called Simon, which before time in the same city used sorcery and bewitched the people of Samaria, giving out that himself was some great one: to whom they all gave heed, from the least to the greatest, saying, 'this man is the great power of God', and to him they had regard, because that of long time he had bewitched them with sorceries."

Not the sort of thing that would endear him to the bishops of the day.

The history of him as related by Justin and by Irenaeus in his work *Adversus Haereses*, tells the story of Simon, who considering himself as God, takes up with a companion called Helen, who was a prostitute in the Phoenician city of Tyre and considered by Simon to be the reincarnation of the female Spirit of Wisdom, Ennoia or Sophia, the "first thought" of the true God.

God, in the form of Simon, working with the goddess figure of Helen, would confer Gnosis upon mankind through their spiritual mystical teachings as the Gnostic sect of the Simonians.

Acts 8:9–24 also portrays Simon as trying to buy the spiritual powers of healing from the apostles Peter and John, the origin of the term Simony, and when this fails, he humbles himself, with the gospel writers making sure that he would always appear inferior to the orthodox apostles.

Even in death, Simon stood no chance with the Christian storytellers.

He is reputed to have died, during a battle of magic with Peter, when Simon, demonstrating his power of flight and levitation, was brought crashing to the ground, when Peter was able to cancel his spell!

Valentinus (circa 100–180 CE) is one of the best-known Gnostic theologians and started his Valentinian school in Rome between 136 CE and 140 CE, reaching the peak of his teaching influence around 150 CE.

Valentinianism became one of the major Gnostic movements and its influence was spread across a huge area, taking in Rome, Egypt, Asia Minor, Syria and North West Africa (*The Economic and Social Origins of Gnosticism*, H.A. Green, Scholars Press, 1985).

Disciples of the faith were still in evidence well into the fourth century, when the Roman Empire was officially Christian, and as is the case with Simon Magus, we learn what we know about the movement, principally from their critics. The usual heresiologists, including the now familiar Irenaeus, were quick to lambast the philosophy with his well-rehearsed diatribes and was joined in the condemnatory language by other Christian writers like Hippolytus of Rome, (circa 170–236 CE), who authored *The Refutation of all Heresies.*

The influence of Valentinus and his alternative view of the Christian message cannot be underestimated. The faith was popular and gained ground rapidly, posing a major thorn in the side of the still developing Catholic Church. Their doctrines, practices and beliefs were totally alien to the politically minded bishops, priests and deacons and had to be refuted and ultimately wiped out. For a time, they were unable to resist its impression on the populace and some great religious philosophers became Valentinians, such as Heracleum, Ptolemy and Theodosius.

The Valentinian philosophy and their religious beliefs were, like other branches of Gnostic Christianity, incredibly complicated systems of thinking and personal dedication, which could only be taught by Gnostic teachers. As we discussed earlier, there was a denial of the God of the Old Testament as the true God and salvation was achieved with the attainment of self-enlightenment or Gnosis and not by faith, something that could not be reconciled by the orthodox fathers.

The concept of Jesus Christ alone, would have had the traditionalists foaming at the mouth.

Jesus was both described as the offspring of the female emanation called Sophia, from the realm of the Pleroma of the true God, and also, in more developed systems of the faith, as the brother and sister relationship, which developed a system of order in the Pleroma.

In reading all this material, it dawned on me very quickly that the Gnostic Christians were no fools and their complex religious systems of whatever group, were cleverly thought-out methods of following a lifelong path of spiritual fulfilment. I noticed, too, how the Gnostic followers were so much more concerned with the teachings of their Jesus figure and the spirituality of the risen Christ and all to be used as a means of raising the psyche to a level of ultimate awareness where the disciple becomes a Christ himself.

I was shocked to observe the huge differences between themselves and their Christian critics and to see Christian texts denying the virgin birth and the resurrection of the flesh, absolutely convinced me that there was more going on in this, the history of the early Church, than I was ever led to believe.

It made me ask myself, just how much more there was to this most intriguing story?

During my early reading, I had only a passing interest in the subject of church history and theology generally but to get to the root of this mystery, I knew I would have to spend some years chasing up all the evidence I could find to answer the basic questions I was beginning to ask myself. The subject became an obsession and as a starting point I thought reading the Gnostic gospels themselves, would be an obvious basis to begin. Little did I realize how long a study that would be in itself.

We do not know who authored these amazing works, but they cast a huge cloud over the argument, if it ever existed, that the early Church was uniform in its beliefs and structure.

The language of these gospels is certainly hard to understand for anybody used to reading the accounts according to Mark or Luke. They speak about attaining illumination and mysterious elements of the cosmos are discussed: Aeons, Archons, Vestures and Pleromas. Previously unknown writings revealed the beliefs about a true God and the condemnation of the Demiurge, false God, Jehovah of the Bible. We learn of female consorts that create the lower world, while others create the angels and we learn, too, about the true nature of Jesus existing as an ordinary human man, and in other readings, as pure spirit.

Some of the texts appear to be gobbledygook but maybe, below the surface of what appears to be nonsense, is a far deeper spiritual secret, still waiting to be understood. Remember, the texts found at Nag Hammadi were written in Coptic, translated from a much earlier version, written in Greek, possibly as early as 80–100 CE. This early Greek version of all the texts may have been more informative to the gospel scholars, as they would have concealed even more secret meanings within the lines of text based on the ancient system of Gematria, whereby sentences contain a series of numbers, which translate into a different meaning. Much more of this later.

The more I researched, the more I realized that I was looking at a faith that was a million miles away from the faith of those that attend my local church every Sunday morning. A faith, a Christianity, that is actually unknown to most people and as such, has no significance. I regularly speak with Church ministers, ordinary priests and vicars, senior church people even students of Divinity and Theology. Virtually none of these groups had anything but a very basic knowledge of the Gnostic story and most, no knowledge at all.

There is something very wrong here. Those ancient Gnostic scribes, who penned their words of divine wisdom, were writing for an enormous group of faithful adherents, who believed the story of their Christ to be just as real as the story being told by the likes of Irenaeus and other bishops of the day.

Who is right in their belief? To look upon the Gnostic gospels as worthless fairy tales, as many orthodox Christians still do, is to deny the brilliant intellect of those spiritually driven truth seekers who taught and led the various Christians of their day.

Their view of the Jesus figure, albeit anathema to the Church today, is as relevant and meaningful, and probably more, than the message conveyed by the composers of Mark, Matthew, Luke and John, whose literal acceptance of the Christ story, did not fit well with the more profound Gnostic philosophy that they practised. Probably, the best-known of the Nag Hammadi find is the Gospel of Thomas, which is essentially a compilation of the sayings of Jesus, many of which, have never been seen before, such as the opening lines:

"Whoever finds the interpretation of these sayings, will not experience death."

A much-quoted line used whenever the Gospel of Thomas is discussed.

This is followed a little later by the lines:

"If those who lead you say to you, 'See, the kingdom is in the sky,' then the birds will precede you. If they say to you, 'It is in the sea,' then the fish will precede you. Rather, the kingdom is inside of you and it is outside of you. When you come to know yourselves, then you will become known, and you will realize that it is you who are the sons of the Living Father. But, if you will not know yourselves, you dwell in poverty and it is you who are that poverty."

The text also records, "These are the secret sayings that the living Jesus spoke and Didymus Judas Thomas recorded." The Doubting Thomas of New Testament fame, supposedly responsible for recording the 114 secret sayings of his teacher, Jesus the Christ.

In a nutshell, Jesus has confirmed that the Gnostic must search for the truth, the meaning, the Christ within himself, where the sacred spark of the divine is waiting to be released.

He tries to teach the notion that the Kingdom of God is not a place where the righteous would be welcomed by the Heavenly Host, or even a symbol of a cataclysmic happening, which the gospels of Mark, Matthew and Luke would have their readers believe.

"His disciples said to him, 'When will the Kingdom come?' Jesus said, 'It will not come by waiting for it. It will not be a matter of saying 'Here it is,' or 'There it is'. Rather, the Kingdom of the Father is spread out upon the earth and men do not see it" (Gospel of Thomas, Nag Hammadi Library, 42:7).

The Kingdom is only achieved via the quest for Gnosis and that kingdom is not something that will arrive in the future, it is achievable in the here and now but only with the guidance of the revealing Logos, the spirit of Jesus the Christ, who declares in the Gnostic text that the follower who becomes as one with the divine within, becomes as one with the Christ himself. The searcher, having found, becomes the equal of the revealing spirit of Jesus and is also a Son of God.

Interestingly, the Thomas of the Gospel of Thomas, Didymus Thomas, is referred to as the "twin" of Jesus, something that the orthodox dismiss out of hand as something that is impossible, because Jesus is never described as having a literal twin in the New Testament.

What it probably relates to is the fact that Didymus Thomas, which means twin, has reached the highest level of Gnosis and was an equal to the Jesus figure and thus they were, in a spiritual sense, one of the same, spiritual twins.

"He who will drink from my mouth will become like Me. I myself shall become he and things that are hidden will be revealed to him" (Gospel of Thomas, Nag Hammadi Library).

The gospel teaches how to know yourself and how to understand the true meaning behind the Kingdom of God.

There is no birth, or life and death story, no stable, virgin or Pontius Pilate. To the writers of this gospel, that storyline had no relevance; they were interested in the spiritual journey made possible through its teachings.

Some scholars suggest that these sayings of Jesus may well have been composed as early as the late first century, in some form. As time progressed, they were added to and changed, as were all religious texts, to accommodate the opinions of the time and indeed, the scribe.

It is also suggested that these sayings may have been part of a very early source known to scholars as Q, from the German Quelle, meaning source.

This document has been suggested as the earliest source of Matthew and Luke, which took their lead from Mark, but additions may be from Q.

However, much scholarly debate rages around this subject, and as no intact copy has ever been found and as a hypothetical text only, it is hard to make any firm assumptions about it.

It should be noted, however, that many of the Gospel of Thomas sayings do appear in very similar form in the New Testament and certainly, in the Gospel of John, which to the avid Bible reader, will be recognized as being a bit different to the other three gospels. In fact, it has an almost Gnostic feel to it.

This gospel is the more spiritual of the four and here, too, Jesus appears as the revealer of the spiritual wisdom and conforms in so many ways to the Gnostic teacher of the alternative gospels.

His Gnostic Christ credentials fail, however, in the fact that the John's gospel relates to Jesus the Logos in a flesh and blood sense, which would in fact be correct if all the Gnostic philosophy of the ancients was as simple as saying that the whole Gnostic belief was based on Christ being totally spirit. It was never as simple as that. Some of those early Christians, heretics to the orthodox, perceived the Messiah as very much flesh and blood but with a very different point of view about his Divinity.

On that basis therefore, the Gospel of John could conceivably be looked at in a Gnostic sense.

Could it be that the Gospel of John was allowed to stay in the official canon because the Gnostic movement was so strong and diverse? A question we may never know the answer to.

This of course does not conform to Valentinian Gnosticism's account of their saviour Jesus Christ. They described Jesus as only appearing to be a physical being and had no belief in his suffering on a cross or bodily resurrection.

You can see as we progress through the early days of the developing Church, just how complicated the Jesus story was for early believers.

A complexity of belief patterns totally unknown to the huge majority of today's Christian followers.

Like me, as you absorb this new information about the origins of the gospel stories and the hugely diverse beliefs that existed at the time, not to mention the inter Christian battles that took place for religious authority, you will begin to ask many deep and probing questions. The answers you will ultimately come up with may surprise you and probably, shock you.

Even now, you know considerably more about the religious chaos of the time, than most of the Christian population today.

There is much more historical detail gathered from centuries of scholarly research and ancient textual evidence still available.

Ask yourself, did you know little or anything about these alternative gospel scriptures? Even now, after only these few pages, has the introduction to the Christians who trod a very different path to the followers of the New Testament, made you think a lot more about the simplicity of the story we were taught at junior school?

When discussing the time of the Gnostic writers we cannot ignore the philosophy and teaching that came out of the highly successful Gnostic school of Marcion.

Around the year 140 CE, Marcion travelled to Rome from his Black Sea home where he began his work on spreading his brand of the Christian message aimed at the Gentile population.

He admired the theology of Paul and declared, like him, that a faith in Christ was essential, not an adherence to the Law.

Like other Christian groups, he too taught that there were two gods, one the true ineffable god of the Pleroma, and the other, the God of the Jews, who was the God of the Old Testament, who was the false God, the God who wanted to trap mankind in the misery and evil of the world we inhabit.

Marcion taught that Jesus, sent by the true God, was not a flesh and blood entity, he only appeared to be of flesh and blood, only appeared to be human. This belief was shared by many other Christians and was later known, as we said earlier, as Docetism.

Why should Marcion revere the writings of Paul in the early days of the Christian struggle?

Well, if we read the works of Paul in Romans 8:3, we see that Paul, like Marcion, makes a point that most readers of the New Testament overlook as not important: Paul says that Christ came "in the likeness of sinful flesh".

This is distinctly Gnostic in its concept, as is the point that Paul makes when he indicates that flesh and blood cannot inherit the Kingdom of God (1 Cor.15:50).

Here, the implication is one of spiritual resurrection of the soul, not a physical resurrection of the body.

There are many elements of the Pauline writings that do give rise to serious questions about Paul's possible Gnostic credentials.

The problems caused by Paul's declaration that flesh and blood could not inherit the Kingdom of God gave our friend Irenaeus huge problems. He is quoted as saying that the heretics used this against the orthodox at every possible occasion.

It is thought that as a result of the weakness in the argument that the orthodox could offer, a Third Epistle to the Corinthians was forged to convey the message that physical resurrection was for real and was a Pauline belief.

So Marcion followed Paul, obviously for a reason. He seemed to appreciate his theology.

Marcion eventually produced a canon of scripture, in fact, a New Testament, which predated the better-known Testament by many years.

This volume was composed of the letters of Paul and surprisingly included an interpretation of the Gospel of Luke but had all the Jewishness of the Old Testament removed. Marcion wanted nothing to do with the Old Testament and its cruel God Jehovah.

How could one compare the loving God of Christ, to the God of the Jews, who throughout the Old Testament, seems to condone all sorts of death and mayhem on the people he falls out with.

The Marcionite church was very successful and flourished right through to the fifth century, when it is recorded that bishops would warn their orthodox followers to beware when in a strange town to make sure that they were not worshiping with heretics (R. Joseph Hoffman, *Marcion: On the Restitution of Christianity*, Wipf and Stock, 2016).

Readers wishing to extend their knowledge of Marcion and indeed all aspects of the little-known gospels, should read the very scholarly but easy to read, work of Bart D. Ehrman, *Lost Christianities: The Battles for Scripture and the Faiths We Never Knew*, OUP USA, 2005.

So, there it is. A subject so great and profound that it would be impossible for us in these pages to give it the time and space it deserves.

Remember this. At the outset of the developing religion, later to be called Christianity, was a series of beliefs, which in the mid first century, was a Judaic Messianic faith that increasingly came under the influence of the Greek philosophical schools.

As time went on, a whole series of different Christian groups developed their own ideas as to what the nature of the Christ story was about.

These groups separated themselves from the orthodox Church and ran in parallel, demonstrating belief patterns that people today find hard to believe.

Most shockingly, Christian people who followed the teachings of their saviour, Jesus Christ, did not believe that he was born of a virgin; a central tenet of the modern Church.

Many did not believe that the Jesus figure was a human at all. He only appeared to be human but was nothing more than pure spirit.

Very many of the alternative Church, those we now call the Gnostics, did not believe in the bodily resurrection of Jesus and thought that those that did believe it were spiritually ignorant.

Christians not believing in the virgin birth and the physical resurrection would not be considered Christian today.

The group of Jesus followers who eventually wrote the early texts of the New Testament, those we call the orthodox, did not themselves mention the virgin birth and somewhat controversially, did not include the resurrection.

This is verifiable if we consult the earliest of the orthodox gospels, the Gospel of Mark, written probably around 70–90 CE but as we said earlier, gospel dating is a very inaccurate science. It is conceivable that the gospels were written at the beginning of the second century CE.

In the Book of Mark there is no mention of a virgin birth, no stables, wise men, difficult inn keepers or passing shepherds and incredibly, in the oldest copies we have of this gospel, the ending appears at chapter 16:8.

The ending simply relates to an empty tomb.

The last twelve chapters, which we are now used to reading, were added at a later date.

This is a very complicated element in the story, and we will look at more of this later.

When even the early New Testament authors do not mention the miraculous birth and the resurrection of the flesh, then something fishy is going on!

As we are discussing the Gospel of Mark, it may be an opportune moment to introduce a bit of a footnote that involves a remarkable group of Christian believers, a Gnostic movement known as the Carpocratians.

The founder of this Christian sect was Carpocrates, who as usual with other Gnostic founders, was vilified by the Church fathers whose views on most religious matters were totally at odds with theirs.

Not surprisingly, this particular school of belief came in for particularly harsh criticism from the usual suspects because much of the Carpocratian way of doing things was based on free love and unbridled licentious behaviour, declaring to their critics that the only way to find the true God was to involve oneself in every kind of bodily experience. Morality and common decency were things they did not recognize. Sexual freedom was the way to God.

In about 200 CE was another of the eminent Church fathers, who was helping develop the orthodox religion and his name was Clement of Alexandria. It was the activities of Clement who is responsible for one of the great mysteries of Christian scholarship. His condemnations of Carpocrates at that time, has left a huge question mark relating to the Gospel of Mark and the Gnostic school that Carpocrates spawned.

It all came to light in 1958, when Morton Smith, a Professor of Ancient History at Columbia University visited the ancient monastery at Mar Saba, not far from Jerusalem, which had been a monastic centre for sixteen hundred years.

While there, he took it upon himself to study the historic library containing ancient texts and manuscripts and was able to find some very interesting material of considerable value to historians.

He came across a very early volume of the works of Ignatius, the well-known Bishop of Antioch, who was making his presence felt around the beginning of the second century CE. At the back of the collection of writings, on blank pages, he discovered something that has shaken the scholarly world to this day.

He was amazed to find a handwritten copy of fragments of a letter reputedly sent from Clement of Alexandria to a friend, Theodore.

The letter, copied by an eighteenth-century scribe, maybe for safekeeping and inserted in the Book of Ignatius, went on to tell that the Gospel of Mark was not the only truth relating to the

Jesus that Mark produced. He explained to Theodore that there was another, more spiritual version of the gospel, known as the Secret Gospel of Mark, which contained storylines not included in the regular version.

Clement quotes two passages that demonstrate this point.

He relates an event in Secret Mark.

The event is similar to the story of Lazarus in John, chapter 11. It tells of the death of a young man in Bethany. The sister of the man begs Jesus to help. A loud voice is heard inside the tomb and Jesus enters and restores the youth to life.

This is followed by:

> The young man looked at him intently and loved him and he began pleading with him that he might be with him. When they came out of the tomb, they went to the young man's house, for he was wealthy.
>
> After six days Jesus gave him a command. When it was evening, the young man came to him, wearing a linen cloth over his naked body. He stayed with him that night, for Jesus was teaching him the mystery of the Kingdom of God. When he got up from there, he returned to the other side of the Jordan.
>
> (This translation taken from the work of author Bart Ehrman in his book *Lost Christianities: The Battles for Scripture and the Faiths We Never Knew*)

Clement's letter also indicates a passage in Secret Mark which is not included in Mark 10:46,

"The sister of the young man whom Jesus loved was there, along with his mother and Salome, but Jesus refused to see them."

What infuriated Clement was that while accepting the Secret Gospel as a very real gospel in the keep of the Church at Alexandria, those nasty Carpocratians had come by a copy of it and had been immediately aware of the homoerotic undertones of the story. Not only that but he indicates that they had even added their own phrase to the gospel; "naked man with naked man".

Clement insisted to Theodore that this was most definitely not included in the Secret Gospel and the Carpocratians were using the gospel and additions of their own, to justify some of their own outrageous activities.

Clement was therefore aware of three versions of the gospel; the orthodox version, the Secret Gospel and the Secret Gospel adjusted by the Carpocratians.

The letter appears to be sent as a result of Theodore's inquiry in how to deal with the Carpocratians and their activities and claims. Clement accuses the Gnostic sect of "mixing the spotless and holy words with utterly shameless lies".

He goes on to advise his friend to never give way when arguing the case against these heretics, as he saw them, and to even deny on oath that the Secret Gospel is by Mark.

It is important to note that in the orthodox Book of Mark there is a story relating to the youth and can be found in Mark 14:51.

Here, the story tells of a bizarre event at the time of Jesus' arrest at Gethsemane.

The guards try to detain a youth who had been following Jesus. As they grab him, the linen cloth covering him comes away and he runs away naked.

An odd thing to add to the story of Jesus' arrest that has never been explained satisfactorily by biblical scholars.

The youth of the Secret Gospel and the youth of Mark 14:51 would appear to have something in common.

Clement's second reference from the Secret Mark regarding Jesus not wanting to meet with the women would actually fit perfectly in the orthodox Mark. At Mark 10:46 the text says:

"And they came to Jericho; and as they went out of Jericho..."

They didn't seem to do much in Jericho. Why should such a meaningless sentence be included?

If on the other hand, the piece from the Secret Gospel is included after "And they came to Jericho", so that it read,

"And they came to Jericho and the sister of the young man whom Jesus loved was there, along with his mother and Salome, but Jesus refused to see them."

It now makes some sense. It is blatantly obvious that something is missing from the version in today's New Testament.

Controversy has raged for years about the letter from Clement, about the Secret Gospel and about the find itself by Morton Smith at the monastery at Mar Saba.

Morton Smith spent many years researching his find. Questions are still asked about whether the scribe forged the whole thing himself and never had a fragment of the supposed letter. Still others questioned whether the insertion at the back of the writings of Ignatius was genuinely from an eighteenth-century hand, or something more recent?

Was the original fragment of Clement's letter a forgery itself? Such is the nature of biblical scholarship, absolutely nothing can be taken for granted.

As well as these questions, we must ask ourselves that if there is a Secret Gospel of Mark, maybe buried deep in the archives of the Vatican, is it possible that it is the original version and the orthodox version was a shortened version, and became the only version allowed for public consumption?

Very few people are even aware of the supposed existence of the Secret Gospel, so for most followers of the faith, the question is purely academic. Scholars, on the other hand, take it far more seriously and are still working on an answer to this enigma.

The Gnostic gospels have provided a wealth of material that points to a time of considerable diversity during those early Christian years of the first, second and third centuries CE and any in-depth study will lead the reader along a route of some very profound soul searching.

In my investigation to establish some facts about the origin of the faith as we know it today and even to establish the validity or not about the very existence of Jesus Christ, then an awareness of the alternative points of view is essential.

I have included them at the start of my quest because it was the remarkable affect they had on me that motivated me into wanting to know more; a lot more, about the most famous man in the world.

Chapter 3

The Enigma of Paul

The goldfish really does think that the whole universe is within the confines of his fish tank. He knows nothing else. The days pass by with everything he needs to do and know within the watery depths of his vitreous home: That is until somebody picks him out of the aquarium, and he looks around himself at the world he never knew.

You can imagine what he might think.

"Holy catfish! What on earth is that?" he thinks, as a giraffe walks past.

He begins to realize, as he splashes back into his water, that there are a lot more things going on around than he ever thought possible. The world he lived in never allowed his knowledge to expand; he simply accepted it as it was.

So it is with us humans. A clever man once said that wise men know that they do not know. Think about that for a moment, because the implication is that there is a world of startling knowledge, not known to us, but maybe common knowledge amongst those who have spent a lifetime within its pages.

It is there for us to share but few of us ever bother. We never step outside the fish tank for a better, more profound view, and so, as we pontificate and express our views with some enthusiasm, we don't see how shallow we are, without the benefit of those unknown elements to the argument.

This philosophy can be applied to any subject and certainly to the subject of the Bible story and the whole concept of early Christianity.

You can imagine our friend the goldfish getting back amongst his pals in the tank and telling them about the animal with the long, very long, neck that happened to pass by when he was visiting this other world!

The other fishes would treat him as though he was a bit odd, while they all got on with their lives in the "real world".

Anybody who thinks that the Jesus story started as simply as the Church would have us think, that is with a miraculous birth of a man whose life we know nothing about until the supposedly historical gospels tell us what happened thirty years later, is very wrong.

The amount of available knowledge relating to the birth of Christianity is enormous but involves investigations into the history of the ancient Egyptians, the ancient Greeks, the Mediterranean mystery religions, the Jewish sect of the Essenes, the politics of the day and so much more; including the Bible stories themselves, examined closely, even studying the original Greek grammar, to reveal truly remarkable elements of the story that I never thought possible.

But possible they are and ancient texts and even stories literally written in stone, on the walls of the Egyptian pyramids, tell us elements of the story that the orthodox Church has conveniently ignored for millennia.

Those of you who read the Bible, maybe only occasionally or maybe regularly, will probably pay little heed to the positioning of the various gospels and letters within its pages.

We often quote the Bible stories of Matthew, Mark Luke and John, followed by Acts and the writings of St Paul.

Why do the accounts of Jesus' life and works appear in this order?

It is accepted almost universally amongst scholars that the Gospel of Mark is the first of the gospels to be written, followed by Matthew and Luke, all three are known together as the Synoptic gospels, because of the similarity of their content. John stands alone as a more spiritual, if not Gnostic gospel.

So, if Mark is the first of the gospels, why does the church allow it to follow Matthew?

Well, to have Mark appear where it should, would be a little inconvenient, because to those who read it closely will know that there is no birth story in the Gospel of Mark. There is no supernatural event involving angels, wise men and a virgin. The story in Matthew, however, does carry the birth story and so would paint a clearer picture for those early readers if they knew how and where their saviour had come from.

Mark begins his tale with the baptism of Jesus by John the Baptist and would thus not really tell the whole story.

In Luke, we find the details are somewhat more comprehensive so by putting Matthew first, it makes the life and times run a little smoother. The early Bible readers needed a birth story to give some historicity to the developing saga.

But what about Paul and his contributions to the New Testament?

Well, this is where things start to get a bit interesting and why I consider St Paul to be a key ingredient in my investigation.

As I have already pointed out, the gospels were written in the order of Mark, Matthew, Luke and John at a non-too specific time at the end of the first century, with John quoted by some as having been composed as late as 140 CE.

Respected scholar Professor Alvar Ellegard, (University of Goteborg, Sweden.), provides impressive evidence for all the gospels having been written after 100 CE.

Clearly, not only do we not know who wrote the gospels, but we really do not know for sure when.

Apologists would have you believe that they were written at a very early date because this gives the account more validity, simply because it was recorded, by word of mouth, much nearer the time.

However, what does seem to be agreed amongst historians is the very early date for the writings of St Paul, maybe in the decade between 50 and 60 CE.

So once again, if Paul is by far the earliest of the writers, why does he have to appear after the fully documented life story of Jesus, almost like an afterthought?

The shrewd editors of our early Bibles knew that by the time the reader had absorbed all the details of the virgin birth, the place it happened, when it happened, the miraculous events, the crucifixion and most tellingly, the resurrection, then the story told by Paul about his conversion, his evangelizing and his visits to meet people who had actually met Jesus, fitted in with the rest of the story, perfectly.

A much closer look at Paul tells a very different story and in so doing, the reader must remember that at his time, there were no gospels written, no Mark, Matthew Luke, or John, so Paul was writing what he knew in his day.

Paul is arguably the most important element in the success of the new religion in the late first century. Without him, the story of Jesus would probably have taken its place alongside all those other mythical mystery religions, so very similar to Christianity in their own way and ultimately have disappeared forever.

Having read the gospels and then gone on to Paul's Epistles, it's easy to look upon Paul as simply one of the evangelists who maintained the storyline of the gospels and went on to do a pretty good job of spreading the word.

However, a closer look at Paul makes him a useful witness in our quest for the real Jesus and where it all came from.

Paul indicates that he was chosen by God to have Christ revealed to him and to be the bearer of good news and also points out that no man had taught him the knowledge, but he had received his revelations through nothing more than visions.

"But I certify you, brethren, that the gospel which was preached of me is not after man. For I neither received it of man, neither was I taught it, but by the revelation of Jesus Christ" (Galatians 1:11–1).

What exactly did Paul know about the life and times of the Son of God who supposedly had walked the earth only a couple of decades before his writing?

Not very much. It is astonishing, when you look for some detail, that he appears to have no knowledge of the virgin birth; this being an essential part of the developing faith.

Throughout his epistles he makes no mention anywhere of Bethlehem or indeed Nazareth.

He has no obvious knowledge of Mary or Joseph; he never mentions them. He appears unaware of the role of John the Baptist and there is not a single mention of any of the miracles. You would think feeding five thousand with a couple of fishes and a few loaves would merit a line or two; he mentions not a word.

St Paul contributes thirteen letters, supposedly penned by himself, although scholars now believe some are forgeries from a later date. In none of these works does Paul indicate his sense of awe or amazement at the wonderful works of his Jesus figure.

Not many people read biblical passages analytically, we simply take them for what they are and assume that they are telling us something that we already know and understand.

Reading Paul and dissecting the content can be mind-blowing when the implications are considered but being able to do this needs a knowledge of so much more than most of us are able to demonstrate.

Without understanding the history of the Gnostics or the early Hellenistic philosophers or understanding the origins and beliefs of the mystical Essenes and Nazarenes, not to mention the politics of the day, we stand no chance at seeing the reality behind the works of St Paul.

Paul's lack of interest in the living Jesus can be hard for a traditional Christian to accept, because it may just mean that he had no knowledge of those events at all! The historical detail of the life of the saviour had not yet been invented when he was spreading the news of his vision of the risen Christ while on the road to Damascus.

It would be easy to argue that there was no need to detail the elements of such a famous life since they were so well known anyway. Well, no, remember Paul himself said that he received no information from man, his revelations of Christ were from God.

And, as we have already mentioned, there were no available New Testament gospels to give a time and place to the story, so we must look closely at the reasons behind this lack of vital knowledge that would undoubtedly have been used in the evangelization, had it been available.

As a reader of the Bible, maybe now or in the past, ask yourself, were you aware of this lack of vital detail in what is the earliest of the testament writings? It is very easy to overlook because of our preconceived ideas about everything we know about the historical Jesus, or think we know.

Does it even matter? Yes, it does. The repercussions could be, and indeed they are, nothing less than earth shattering.

Anybody trying to sell their new religion to a diaspora, or dispersed group of Hellenized Jews and Gentiles would certainly have used as much ammunition as possible to make their story more convincing. Especially so, when Paul tells us that he had met Peter, James, and John in Jerusalem. Surely, they who had reputedly walked with Jesus during his ministry, would have provided so much material for Paul to use, he really would not know where to begin.

Paul would certainly have wanted to know the story of the divine birth, for this was the obvious stamp of authority from God. He would have sat in amazement at the stories of the miracles and the parables would have been a must for his proselytizing around the diaspora.

John the Baptist, the spirit of prophecy of the Old Testament would be an essential element in the development of the story because he, in the New Testament, is made to fulfil the prophecies of the Old Testament and announce to the world the arrival of the Messiah (Isaiah 40:3–5).

Nothing predicted in the Old testament is merely a prediction that may or may not come about. They were looked upon as truths that would certainly be fulfilled, and those early predictions would come in very handy at a much later date in the composition of the gospels.

How on earth could Paul ignore the hapless villain Pontius Pilate? Actually, he doesn't. In 1 Timothy Chapter 6:13 he talks about Jesus and Pilate. But hold on, that particular letter is considered not to be genuine and probably an interpolation of a later date and is now considered a definite forgery.

For the record, only the works in Romans, Galatians, 1 Thessalonians, 1 and 2 Corinthians and Philippians, are considered to be the genuine letters of Paul (Prof. Alvar Ellergard, University Goteborg, Sweden).

The forgeries do carry a Christian message of the time but a time somewhat later than when Paul was at work, so they cannot help us here in the enigma of missing detail.

Incredibly, it's a startling fact, that Paul's theology is based, almost totally, on the crucifixion and the resurrection, to the point that some scholars refer to his beliefs as "Crosstianity". He is only interested in the risen Christ, not Jesus the man.

Having said that, does he include in his writings any useful information about where the crucifixion took place or, most tellingly, when?

No, not a word is offered to fill in these gaps. Paul is ignoring these essential elements, to the astonishment of most orthodox Catholic scholars, for a reason.

As we have suggested, he knew nothing about them!

The proof is in the proverbial pudding. Take a long look at the Letters of Paul and you will realize that what we have indicated above is correct and the significance of this is that it opens a whole can of worms about the truth behind the origins of early Christianity and the life of Jesus, and ignoring the fact will not take away the huge significance.

Professor Alvar Ellegard in his remarkable work, *Jesus –*

One Hundred Years Before Christ: A study In Creative Mythology,
confronts this problem head on.

In his book, the depth of Testament analysis with meticulously
listed source material, is obviously based on sound scholarship.

The point he makes is that Paul pays no attention to any
of the essential elements of the story and is interested only in
the fact that his Jesus is resurrected and is in Heaven with the
Father; he interprets his dreams or visions as a sign that the
Messiah is preparing to come to earth for the much-expected
Last Judgement.

Ellegard goes on to make a remarkable claim and one that
with the body of evidence he provides, suggests that the Jesus
of Paul's theology was a timeless being, a spirit of a God or a
man that could have existed at any time in the past!

This is a mind-blowing theory and one that any orthodox
church member will find impossible to comprehend, unless
that is, they expand their mind and take in some of the other
historical detail surrounding Paul, that makes this assessment
very possible indeed.

Of course, traditional followers of the faith will not do this. Can
you imagine the bishop of your local diocese taking an unbiased
view of a storyline that would and probably will, change the
whole concept of how the history of Jesus came about?

No, I think not either. When I dug deep into the Pauline
Epistles, many years ago, I, too, noticed huge holes in the text,
which left me wondering what was going on under the surface.

As my knowledge and awareness of the relevant history of
the time grew considerably, the concept of a timeless being who
had been around as a real human being many years before or
even centuries before, struck me as a real possibility too.

This would change the face of Christianity forever!

But what of the Pauline passages that seem to have a real time
factor in the life and death of his visionary, spiritual Christ?

The obvious, much quoted passage is that from 1 Cor.15:3,

where Paul tells of the resurrected Jesus who rose again on the third day, "according to the scriptures", again calling on the Old Testament prophecy as a truth. But the main point is that he claims the risen body was witnessed by "above five hundred brethren at once, of whom the greater part remain unto this present, but some are fallen asleep."

The problems here become, as usual, a little difficult.

Obviously, we are not told where or when the magnificent spectacle was witnessed.

Was it another case of visionary appearances to the believers at a much, much later date? Were all the apostles, not Disciples, convinced by visions that they were as one with the Christ? Was it a case of mass hysteria? Did it actually happen?

Another obvious question to ask is why the five hundred are not identified, at least by place, and why no mention of the most incredible appearance of all time, in the gospels. Not a word is included in the gospels or Acts. The five hundred were soon forgotten. This is deeply suspicious.

Who were these 500, why did they not make one huge fuss about the miraculous event? Indeed, was Paul amongst them or is he talking simply from hearsay. Did any of the witnesses leave any written history about their experience? Again no, not a word in history from any of the historians who were writing at the time.

Did Paul think it might make a good point to the people of Corinth who could not verify the story anyway? Hmmm... this may just be possible.

What did Paul say in his New Testament Letter to the Romans?

In Romans 3:7 he shamelessly declares, "But if through my falsehood God's truthfulness abounds to his glory, why am I still being condemned as a sinner, and why not say (as some people slander us by saying that we say), 'Let us do evil so that good may come'? Their condemnation is deserved."

In a word, stretching the facts a bit, adding a bit here and there or downright lies, does not really matter if it furthers the cause of the Lord!

This supposed concrete proof of the Pauline Messiah having resurrected is not a very convincing confirmation.

You must agree, it is a question well worth asking if we are to come to any serious conclusions and faith alone is not a good enough answer.

There is more to this story than meets the eye.

As I keep pointing out and probably will continue to do so, to understand anything about what is going on in the pages of the Bible, so much more associated knowledge is an essential.

With this in mind, the reader of the New Testament should be aware that Philosophy and Religious scholars have been aware for many years that Buddhism has had a major influence on the formation of many of the gospel stories, which was something that stunned me, when I first realized this.

The late Danish scholar and expert on ancient Sanskrit, Dr Christian Lindtner (1949–2020) perceives the gospels to be so similar in content that he suggests they are almost a direct lift from the original ancient Buddhist texts.

Dr Burkhard Scherer, of Canterbury Christ Church University, (http://www.kibi-edu.org/prof-dr-b-scherer) says, "It is very important to draw attention on the fact that there is Buddhist influence in the gospels." He does not agree, however, to the extent that Dr Lindtner suggests but joins many other historians when he adds, "There is much Buddhist stuff going on in the gospels."

That great scholar of the Gnostic gospels that we referred to earlier, Professor Elaine Pagels of Princeton University, has written, "one need only listen to the words of the Gospel of Thomas, [Nag Hammadi Library], to hear how it resonates with the Buddhist tradition."

This is another vital point in our ever more complicated

quest and to dismiss the findings of the world of academia as meaningless and insignificant, as most of the Orthodox authorities do, is something akin to a belief in the flat earth.

We will be returning to this fascinating subject and its effect on the Jesus story, a little later.

The point to be made here, is that Buddhism is very evident in the New Testament and when Paul makes his claims, without any obvious foundation or historical detail, then we can look for the origins of the myth elsewhere.

Dr Lindtner goes to great lengths in his work to demonstrate the very same story in the early Buddhist texts where five hundred monks witness the cremation of the physical body of their Lord who goes up to the world of Brahmā in the flames; that's to say, they witnessed their "raised" Lord.

As we will discuss later, it is a fact that there was much Eastern influence in and around Alexandria during the early years of the first century, as a result of the developing trade routes.

On reflection then, Paul's story of the five hundred does not sound too convincing if we are delving deep for more substance than mere faith.

His reference to telling a few lies to enhance the glory of God, (Rom. 3:7) does not fill me with confidence. Where did he get that idea from? Guess what? According to Dr Lindtner, in the Buddhist Lotus Sutra, their missionaries are advised to do exactly the same: employ tricks and lies for the greater glory of the Buddhas.

The other passage that is much quoted as a real time event and a real happening, is the taking of the bread and wine, represented in the Synoptics as the Last Supper.

Paul again, when read closely, says he gets this information directly from the Lord, that is, another visionary experience.

There was nothing new about ritual meals at the time of Paul's mission. They were centuries older than the new faith of the Christians. It was common amongst many of the so-called Mystery Religions of the day.

"He who will not eat of my body, nor drink of my blood so that he may be one with me and I with him, shall not be saved."

Familiar words and obviously spoken by the Lord Jesus Christ? No, these are the words supposedly used in the worship of the much older Saviour God Mithras (M. J. Vermaseren, *Mithraic Communion, Mithras,* "The Secret God", Barnes and Noble, 1963).

The world St Paul moved in and the religions he was very aware of, would mean that there was nothing original about a ritual meal. It could have been part of the ceremonial procedure of the Church he was associated with, the Church of God, but not related to the Jesus figure of the gospels.

I never realized just what significance Paul, or Saul in his previous pre-Jesus existence, had had on the development of the Faith as it unfolded over the decades.

It is a startling fact, that without his original vision, the new religion would not have spread in the diaspora and having spread, gone on to form what we now know as the Catholic Church. It would have quite literally taken its place with all the other cults of the day and "withered on the vine".

One vision from a man we know little about, results in one of the most powerful religious movements, lasting till the present day. Remember, the gospels were created much later, as a direct result of his vision and dream.

The more I probed the history of Paul and looked at the times he lived, including the Church and religions he was familiar with, it became blindingly obvious that all was not as smooth as the Church would have liked it to have been in those very early days.

Paul's home was reputedly Tarsus in Asian Minor or modern-day Turkey. As a centre of intellectual excellence, he would have been closely associated with the Hellenistic practices going on around him. These philosophies would naturally have affected his view of the world and he would have been aware of the religious elements that appealed to the populous.

Equally, as a Jew, probably a Pharisee, he was determined to defend the purity of his beliefs, but that changed. Some scholars are not entirely convinced that Paul was a Jew!

Known then as Saul, we are told in Acts 26:10 that he was more than enthusiastic in his persecution of the developing cult of Christians.

"I put many in prison and when they were put to death, I cast my vote against them."

In Acts, too, after overseeing the stoning of Stephen, we are told that Saul immediately went on to persecute the members of the Church in Jerusalem and while Stephen was being buried by apostles of the Church, "Saul was ravaging the Church by entering house after house; dragging off both men and women, he committed them to prison" (Acts 8:3).

Suddenly, everything changes for Saul. For some reason and of course, we will never know the reality behind this, he has a vision, a revelation that turns his whole life around. Saul, now calling himself Paul, begins his evangelization and hails the vision as a sign that the end of times was near and the Messiah, in the name of Jesus or Yeshua in the original Hebrew, would usher in the Messianic age of global and universal peace.

The word Messiah then meant the anointed one and initially referred to a human leader, a leader so powerful that evil and tyranny would not be able to stand before his leadership.

He would be descended from the line of David and would rule and unite the people of Israel.

The Jews were desperate for this Messiah as the Greek and Roman rule over the years had become ever more intolerable; as they thought more and more about this, they considered his arrival imminent, and they knew that as according to the scriptures, that eternal religious concept that everything was based on, he would certainly demonstrate a CV as depicted in the many verses relating to him in the Book of Isaiah, 11:4, 11:1, 53:7, 11:10 and many more.

Well, Paul has his dream of the man construed by him as the Messiah, but he took it a little further.

Paul perceived the Jewish Messiah as the Hellenistic Christ, and this gave his Messiah a far more divine nature: one that had died as an offering to a divine being as a sacrifice in return for the absolution of the sins of the people and their everlasting salvation.

When Paul began to spread his "good news", the fledgling Christian Church was already in existence and the followers of that church had their own views about their faith.

We can see from Paul's letters that he is frequently having to defend himself against other supposed Christians who do not see the message in the same way that Paul does.

Paul was changing the basic nature of what many of them stood for. He was taking away the Jewishness of the religion and allowing the Greek Hellenistic influence to move in.

We know from what we read that Paul had no interest in the sayings or works of Jesus. Did his opponents think that his theology was the wrong way round? Maybe they saw the works and ministry of God's Son as more important than Paul's "cross-tianity" and his adherence to the raised Christ and the spiritual Jesus.

In a strange way, it's true to say that Paul's dreams and visions opened up a whole can of worms!

Paul fell out with the pillars of the early church, the apostles, Peter, James and John.

They, like many others of the early Jewish followers, were not at all happy about Paul inviting Gentiles to enter the Church and disregard the basic tenets of Judaism, such as circumcision and dietary rules. The Mosaic Law was critically important to those very early Jews, but probably not all.

There was a huge amount of diversity, argument and counter argument going on, immediately after Paul's revelations, which he conceived as the one true Christ, and went about letting everybody else know it too!

I was amazed when I learned about this diversity and real animosity. I had always believed that Christianity developed from a true revelation from God and the gospel stories had developed a life story, historically correct in every way.

It really didn't happen like that! The historical reality is so much more complex and as we pointed out earlier, totally unknown to the not too profound reader of the New Testament.

Paul was directing his new message to the Jews far away in the diaspora and to the Gentiles as well, in places like Corinth, and Antioch, where like Jews everywhere at the time, thought the time had come to escape the discrimination which they considered had gone on long enough.

As we have already pointed out, not all the Jews he approached agreed with his ideas about the Messiah.

The idea of a supernatural superhero did not fit well with many of the groups whose Messiah was of an earthlier nature.

However, there were groups of Messianic Jews, essentially in the diaspora, who were open to his religious message and again, by relating to the scriptures of the Old Testament, were able to relate to the figure revealed to Paul.

Paul knew how to sell his product and he knew full well that there were ready takers who would fulfil his ambition to spread a completely different type of Messianic faith, not only in the outlying areas of the Jewish diaspora but in Jerusalem itself.

Paul, like we said, had many clashes with those he opposed, and the major bust up with Peter, one of the central figures from the Church at Jerusalem, a pillar of the community, was about the dietary rules.

The story is described in Galatians 2:1–14 and ends up with Paul calling Peter a hypocrite and probably more.

It was not long after this that it appears that Paul dedicated his mission to the Gentiles, primarily. Jewish converts would obviously have been amongst them too.

Equally, he appears to leave the ministry directed towards the Jews in Jerusalem to the leadership of Peter, described to us in the New Testament as the apostle of Jesus.

It's at this point that it should be realized that any one element of my investigation so far could be a subject of considerable study in itself.

Paul's links with the Jerusalem Church and his discourses with their leaders, the so-called apostles, Peter, and James, have occupied the time and pages of many scholars' theses and their findings have had considerable significance on the understanding of what was going on at the time.

Similarly, I could add pages to my own inquest if I were to follow up the work and letters of Paul as he moved around the diaspora. We could analyse his writings that reflect the developing Christian message in and around the Aegean Basin.

We could talk at length about his work at Ephesus, one of the most important developing centres of commerce and philosophy in all of Asia.

These are incredibly important elements in the story of the creation of the New Testament and indeed as a prophet for the very new Jesus movement, he was a founding figure for the resulting gospels, albeit through a very circuitous route.

"[I]t's Paul who starts the writing of the New Testament by writing letters to these fledgling congregations in the cities of the Greek East" (Prof L. Michael White, Director of the Religious Studies Programme at University of Texas, Austin).

With that in mind, that simple paragraph relating to Paul being the founding creator of the ultimate book we call the New Testament, resonates with a lot more significance than at first appears.

I suspect that you, like me, read the Bible many years ago,

assuming the Letters of Paul were written at a time that the gospels were common knowledge to the early Christians, who had adopted the faith.

In fact, taking Paul as the early Testament founder, it is self-evident that the life story of Jesus Christ, with all the romanticised ingredients of births, sayings and miracles had still not been developed for common consumption.

Amazingly, Paul's dream or vision or supernatural revelation was all there.

The supernatural character he had introduced as the redeemer, the faith in whom promised salvation and everlasting life based on his sacrificial death, was at that time a divine being without any real history.

How then did the visionary figure, revealed in the mystical vision of a man whose motives we do not know, develop from the purely spiritual being of Paul's resurrected Messiah to become the Christ Saviour who was born of a virgin, was fathered by the Jewish sky God, walked on water, raised the dead, came back to life after his own death and left us with the best-known life story on earth?

Paul knew none of this. It still had not been written.

Even if there was an oral tradition of the divine works, why was none of it mentioned by Paul during his sojourns to the communities of Corinth, Ephesus and others? Here is a man who has a blinding supernatural vision, takes it on himself to evangelize about the message as he sees it, changes the nature of the Jerusalem Church and its followers by implying that the Mosaic Law was no longer necessary and in the eyes of many Jews, arrogantly develops a divine Christ, based on his understanding.

To understand anything about the Jesus story, its origins and ultimate development into the twenty-seven books of the New Testament, we should look a lot closer at the nature and indeed, identity of Paul's Damascus vision and, also, we must examine very closely, the very nature of that early Christian church called by most scholars, the Church of God and most tellingly, the nature of the Jewish sect that was associated with it.

To do this, I will need to investigate a lot more about the philosophies and religions that proliferated at the time of his travels in the middle of the first century. I will come back to him and ask serious questions about that vision and his fellow apostles at the Church of God.

Chapter 4

The Mystery Religions

If what you have read so far has opened your eyes to the simple fact that there is a lot more to our Christian origins than what you first thought, then prepare to be surprised, shocked or totally disillusioned, depending on your attitude to the Bible Story, when you understand more about the world and religious mix that Paul and the people he preached to, were used to.

The Roman Empire during the time of Paul, the Church of God and the people who later wrote the gospels, was a time of great peace and prosperity, introduced by the Emperor Augustus in about 27 BCE and lasted for nearly two hundred years.

In was in this climate that the civilisations of the Greeks, the Romans, the Egyptians, the Persians and certainly, India were able to mix in one huge melting pot and share ideas, philosophies and significantly, religions at a time of relative tolerance, where freedom of religious thought was usually acceptable if it didn't upset the Roman applecart.

By the first century CE, major centres like Alexandria in Northern Egypt had become thriving centres of trade and learning, involving different nationalities from all over the Empire.

Alexandria became one of the great historical centres of the ancient world. Founded in 332 BCE by Alexander the Great, it set the foundations for civilisation and learning and under his successors, the Ptolemies, the Jews who had moved from their homeland to live there were allowed a considerable degree of political independence and were even allocated areas of the city for their community to live, to maintain the purity of their laws and not be influenced by local cultic beliefs.

The city produced great thinkers and writers. The first-century scientist Hero who studied steam power, was a famous citizen, as was the great physician Galen.

The city attracted some of the greatest philosophers of the ancient Empire, who went on to leave their mark on the foundations of Christianity.

Philo was a Jewish author and philosopher from a very wealthy and influential Alexandrian family, who as a student of the philosophy of Plato would go on to mix his Hellenistic thinking with that of his traditional Jewish belief with some interesting results on the early Christian church.

The city is well known for so many things but as a centre of ancient learning, the great library at Alexandria was supposedly, truly remarkable.

With hundreds of thousands of scrolls in its keep, it represented the centre of educational excellence in the ancient world.

Existing historical written evidence gives only small clues to the size and magnificence of the library and also little is known about its ultimate destruction.

Plutarch, one of the renowned historians of the early second century, circa 118 CE, tells us simply that the library was destroyed by fire and some reports tell of a great fire in the city caused by the invasion of Julius Caesar in 47 BCE.

A smaller library, housed in the Temple dedicated to Serapis, lived on into the Christian period, and in the year 391 CE persecution of anything non-Christian had reached new levels; the pagan temple of Serapis was fair game for the city's Christian Patriarch, Theophilus, who duly set about destroying everything therein, statues, books, scrolls and, of course, people.

It was recorded by the historian Socrates Scholasticus.

"[T]hen he destroyed the Serapeum [a temple] and the bloody rites of the Mithreum, he publicly caricatured. The Serapeum also he showed full of extravagant superstitions and he had the phalli of Priapus carried through the midst of the forum" (Socrates Scholasticus).

He goes on to describe the utter destruction conferred on this centre of learning by the ignorant mob.

The great works of Persian, Greek, Egyptian and Roman scholars were lost forever; works relating to science, architecture, poetry, mythology, and religious tradition, all lost to history.

"The real tragedy of course is not the uncertainty of knowing who to blame for the library's destruction but that so much of ancient history, literature and learning was lost forever" (Preston Chesser, Ohio State University).

It seemed opportune to mention in some detail the story of the greatest ancient store of knowledge, because it brings home the point that the peoples who composed the civilisation of the time of Jesus Christ were not the ignorant pagan peasants who would be saved by the unique, one-off revelation of the saving Christ, but were highly educated, deeply spiritual, creative people, who were responsible, as we said earlier, for some of the most incredible architecture of the era, not to mention the literature of Homer and the Greek myths, that we still read in the present day.

The Egyptians were masters of mathematics and geometry, they must have been to have built the complex pyramids.

The ancient Greeks lived by numbers in their philosophy, as put forward by Pythagoras.

Socrates, Plato and Philo Judaeus were philosophers and writers whose work we revere to this day.

Their religions, too, were deeply spiritual and had seemingly fused together from their ancient origins in Egypt, Persia, and Greece.

Centres of worship to these ancient gods would have been well known to Paul and the people he was approaching with his new message, all over the lands of the Jewish diaspora, not just Alexandria.

You can imagine preachers on soap boxes on every street corner, extolling the virtues of their saving superhero, while the traditional Jewish thinker would have none of it.

The mighty gods of the Hellenistic Empire, Zeus, Apollo, and Hermes, were looked upon in a more mythical sense as opposed to the far more personal gods that had found their way into the developing civilisation, and it was in this environment that the new God figure, Jesus, had to compete for the attentions of the multitude, via the efforts of Paul in the mid first century and the gospel writers, bishops and Church fathers of the second century CE.

Throughout the centuries, the composite lands of Egypt, Persia and Greece had developed remarkably advanced societies, all of whom had created their own god figures based on the same basic underlying concept of death and rebirth, which in the earliest days, would have reflected the life and death and life again of the vegetative cycle.

Students of the ancient religions are fully conversant with the names of these gods and we, if we are to understand more about the concepts of early Christianity, should know them too.

The very well-known god and goddess of Egypt, Osiris and Isis, are recorded as far back as 2000 BCE and scholars have suggested as far back as 3100 BCE (Veronica Ions, *Egyptian Mythology*, 1968).

The cult grew into an enormously influential belief and spread across the borders into the Greek and Roman Empires.

The Greeks had their pantheon of gods including the important god Dionysus whose cult had conquered the whole of Greece by the sixth century BCE.

The cult of Adonis was widespread too, having originally developed in Phoenicia.

One of the greatest competitive god figures to challenge the Jesus cult was the Persian god Mithra, who was adopted by the Roman Empire as Mithras, although some scholars declare that the direct link is not certain.

"In the Roman Empire, this same deity was called Mithras and was the central figure of a mystery religion that for almost five hundred years vied with Christianity for dominance" (*Mithras: Mysteries and Initiation Rediscovered*, D. Jason Cooper, Red Wheel/Weiser,1996).

Centuries before this, the Persians revered their prophet, Zarathustra, who gave rise to the cult of Zoroaster, the importance of which in the origins of world religions, cannot be overstated.

"Zarathustra is the most important person in the recorded history of religion, bar none. The first man to promulgate a divinely revealed religion. He influenced the religions of Judaism, Christianity, Mithraism, Islam, Northern Buddhism, Manicheism and the pagan Norse Myths" (Cooper).

Attis, Orpheus, Persephone, Demeter, Serapis, Ishtar and Asherah too, all played their part in the enormous spiritual melting pot, which was present at the time of the creation of the Jesus story.

These profoundly spiritual and deeply philosophical beliefs, which were associated with the various deities, have given rise to their description as Mystery Religions.

The legendary poet, musician and prophet of ancient Greek belief was the revered figure of Orpheus, whose cult following gave rise to the Orphic Mysteries, from which so much of the philosophy of the mystery religions developed.

The cult of Orpheus promised an eternal life in another world and was responsible for the concept of the divine spirit trapped within mankind, which we discussed earlier when we noted that the Gnostic Christians used the spirit of the Christ to reach the inner soul and discover gnosis and the oneness with the divine.

So it was, too, with the Orphics who taught that the spirit of the divine was trapped within man in the form of the man god Dionysus and just like the later Gnostic Christians, they taught how to achieve oneness and possess eternal life. The Gnostics who took up Christianity and practised it in their own way, had a lot in common with the more ancient Orphics.

The followers of the many cults could relate their beliefs to any of the other religious paths because they shared so many common ideas.

The stories of their gods and the belief patterns were meant to be looked at on two different levels. There was the outer story, or a literal belief in the story and its supernatural content and there was a far more spiritual way of looking at it, a way open only to those who had been initiated in the secrets and the meanings on a deeper level.

These mysteries were absorbed and understood by some of the greatest philosophers of the empire and were shared by the common people and the finest brains of the day. The mystery schools and centres of religious practice were scattered all over the lands of the Mediterranean.

Initiates had to work at their beliefs before they could expect to understand the deeper allegorical meanings of the superficial myth and only when they were spiritually ready, were they allowed to know the secrets of the inner sanctum.

This may sound a little familiar to you if you cast your mind back to the philosophical path taken by those Gnostic Christians, who using allegorical teachings of the Jesus figure, were able to find the truth of the Christ within and discover true Gnosis.

The educated initiates knew they were dealing with a perennial myth relating to their deity and indeed every other resurrecting deity that they were aware of but it was the spiritual journey that mattered and the subsequent oneness with the divine.

Remember, the concept of Gnosis, that is the search for enlightenment, was not only a philosophy associated with those early Christians which we described earlier, but a profound thinking system that went back to the early days of the Greek Empire and arguably, before that.

A minor deity of a particular region would be elevated hugely to a much higher level of adoration when the godly attributes that were so well known, were introduced.

Dionysus, for example, developed from a minor god figure, a god of wine and the vine, into a highly influential god when the philosophy of the mysteries was explained.

The gods, too, shared many names and were as we explained, easily interchangeable.

The scholar Dr Martin Alfred Larson (1897–1994) says that the ancient historian Herodotus (484 BCE–425 BCE) would use the names of Osiris and Dionysus interchangeably. Depending, too, on where the religion was followed, the different cultures gave rise to different versions of the basic concepts behind the myth.

Thus, the myth of Dionysus, for example, is described differently in other parts of the ancient world. His birth is described as having been from a mortal woman, Semele, who was impregnated by the Olympian god Zeus; in another form, the great god Zeus, fathers the child via Persephone the goddess.

His death, too, is altered according to the origin of the story, but the overriding factor in all of this is that the general motif relating to the myriad of dying and resurrecting gods, coming back to life sometimes by rebirth, is followed throughout the allegorical myth.

Festivals to celebrate their deities were elaborate affairs and probably none greater than the celebrations at the Eleusinian Mysteries, which, maybe surprisingly, are quite well documented in their details.

We hear of thousands of worshippers parading through the streets at its site near Athens, marching to the Great Hall of Initiation, where they were met by the Hierophant, the Priest or Priestess and then amid the cacophony of gongs, chanting and incredibly bright light, the secrets of the rituals were revealed, and the celebrants sworn to secrecy about what they had experienced.

Archaeology and artefacts with depictions of the event have

given us much information.

There is no lack of documents for the cult of Eleusis. On the contrary, no other local cult in Greece is so richly attested. The sanctuary itself, which Pausanias demurred to describe, is there for all to see, thanks to careful excavations. The great hall of initiation, the Telesterion, and its development from the Peisistratean to the Parthenon era are particularly well known, as are the strange, asymmetrically placed holy of holies and the throne of the hierophant.
(*Homo Necans: The Anthropology of Ancient Greek Sacrificial Ritual and Myth*, Walter Burkert, Translated by Peter Bing, University of California Press, 1986)

The Eleusinian Mysteries were in honour of the goddesses Demeter and Persephone, sometimes mother of Dionysus, whose presence at the celebrations was confirmed by the great mythologist of modern times Carl Kerenyi. "The hierophant at Eleusis appears as a second Dionysus."

In another of his works, Kerenyi makes the very significant point, "Dionysus, the archetypal image of indestructible life" (*Eleusis: Archetypal Image of Mother and Daughter*, Carl Kerenyi, Princeton University Press, 1991).

These theatrical displays of worship in the secret places of initiation and revelation were mirrored in other places where the celebrants would, like at Eleusis, take part and share in what amounted to the passion of their deity.

Herodotus, (484 BCE–425 BCE) reports in his tome *The Histories* that he was present at a mystery festival when he was travelling in Egypt.

The story is recorded by Sir James Frazer in his book *The Golden Bough*.

Herodotus tells us that the grave of Osiris was at Sais in

Lower Egypt and that there was a lake there upon which the sufferings of the god were displayed as a mystery by night. This commemoration of the divine passion was held once a year: the people mourned and beat their breasts as if to testify their sorrow for the death of the god. (*The Golden Bough: A Study in Religion and Magic,* Sir James George Frazer, Dover Publications Inc. 2003)

The mystery religions were certainly popular and provided all the spiritual needs of the time.

But it was the pattern of belief of the various traditions that really upset the Church fathers of the second century, who by now, had copies of the gospel stories, which at last, had provided a historical life and works of their Jesus.

Even as the Church tried to propagate their Saviour story, the pagans who adhered to the original old religions, were critical in their observations. Celsus, the second-century intellectual Platonic philosopher and satirist was one of many who perceived the obvious links with the life stories and passion of deities like Osiris, Dionysus and Mithras.

Celsus is quoted as saying,

Are these distinctive happenings unique to the Christians – and if so, are they unique? Or are ours to be accounted myths and theirs believed? What reasons do the Christians give for the distinctiveness of their beliefs? In truth, there is nothing at all unusual about what the Christian believes, except that they believe it to the exclusion of more comprehensive truths about God.

(Celsus, *On Christianity*)

Celsus was not a popular chap amongst the early Church writers and especially a third-century Church father called Origen of Alexandria whose acclaimed work *Contra Celsum* (248 BCE) gives us plenty of information about Celsus and his works.

Like Irenaeus before him, who gave us much detail about the alternative Christians, the Gnostics, Origen tells us much about Celsus as he tries to dissect and refute the accusations that are made about the Christian faith.

Other Church leaders such as Justin Martyr (circa 100–165 CE) found it almost impossible to answer some of the similarity problems and commented,

> When we say that Jesus Christ was produced without sexual union, was crucified and died, and rose again, and ascended to heaven, we propound nothing new or different from what you believe regarding those whom you call the sons of Jupiter. (Justin Martyr, *First Apology*, Chapter 1)

He wrote, too, that it was the Devil himself who had created these similarities:

"For when they say that Dionysus rose again and ascended to Heaven, is it not evidence that the Devil has imitated the prophecy?" (Justin Martyr from *Dialogue with Trypho*, Chapter 16).

(It should be mentioned that some scholars debate the actual wording of this piece and using it in a shortened form has altered the original meaning.)

What was it then, about these mystical philosophies and religious beliefs, that so upset the Christian founders of the second and third centuries?

The word "Syncretism" is defined as: "The attempted reconciliation or union of different or opposing principles, practices or parties, as in philosophy or religion".

Remember this word, because as we continue our observations, it becomes more and more obvious just how this word and definition demonstrates itself throughout the history of the world's religions.

We have already seen how the basic elements of the mystery

religions began to fuse together and create a perennial myth that had a profound significance in the hearts and souls of their followers.

The very earliest civilisations perceived the rising Sun as their sacred deity in all parts of the developing world. These beliefs were remarkably similar, even for those who lived thousands of miles apart and could not normally have shared their beliefs personally.

The life story of the Sun developed naturally and had a common thread, as did the myths of the dying and resurrecting saviours of the Mediterranean. But, before the deity died, he or she had to be born and the holy birth stories are abundant.

Most of us are aware of the basic details of the supposed historicity of the birth of Jesus.

Born of a virgin and fathered by the Jewish tribal God of the Old testament, without any sexual necessities, the child was brought forth in a stable.

We read of the presence of wise men who come from the east bearing gifts and, of course, there is the star that leads them to the birth site. The very nasty Herod even ordered the massacre of all the innocent children at the time, to prevent the Messiah causing him some serious problems. We must not forget the angel who announced the whole of this miraculous episode to the incredulous Joseph.

All this is a unique supernatural happening, which has become one of the main foundations of the Christian religion and is celebrated annually at Christmas to reinforce the importance and magnificence of the revealing event.

However, there are more than a few problems associated with this story that must be confronted and considered.

Like so many elements of the gospel narratives, much of it develops as a result of Old Testament prophecies, and stories are based on the underlying prediction, simply because it had to.

As we discussed earlier, an Old Testament prophecy was not just a probable happening, it was a truth. It would happen and that is something the gospel writers knew only too well. They would turn to the Hebrew Bible at any possible chance to make a story fit the myth, which they wanted to create.

The prophecy that gave rise to the wording of the miraculous birth in Matthew 1:23 comes from the Old Testament Book of Isaiah 7:14, "A virgin shall conceive."

When the original wording for this was translated from the old Hebrew into the Greek, at the time of the writing of the Septuagint, the Old Testament in Greek, which was probably the source material for the scholar who penned the words of Matthew, the word for virgin was a mistranslation.

The translator had defined the Hebrew word almah, to mean "virgin", when in fact it means "young woman".

The correct word in Hebrew, and it is used in several places in the Old Testament to mean "virgin", is betulah.

This is now so well known that some versions of the Bible make a footnote for the reader to indicate the error.

For example, in the Contemporary English Version, we read, "a virgin is pregnant" and then there is a footnote to inform the reader that the Hebrew word did not imply a virgin birth. Young woman is given as an alternative.

In other versions, such as the Revised Standard Version, they do not bother with the virgin wording at all and go straight to "a young woman shall conceive".

Could the whole concept of a virgin conceiving the Holy Child be based on a simple error of translation?

Were the Matthew and Luke versions of the birth story as unique as orthodox Christians believe, as a main tenet of their faith?

It is certainly interesting that Mark, the first of the gospel writers, does not include a birth history in his writings. Why not? Obviously we do not know the answer to this, but it would seem to indicate that maybe he knew he was on shaky ground, because there was still no official history composed to give a birth narrative. It is only in Matthew and Luke where we can find passages that fulfil the need for an historical setting for the miraculous birth of the Saviour.

At the time of the writing of the gospels, just about every deity that was known to the man in the street could demonstrate either a supernatural birth where the sacred child was born to a mortal woman and fathered by one of the gods or, in several other cases, born of a virgin and again fathered by a well-known god figure.

It was as though any god who was going to make any impression, certainly needed a virgin birth in their curriculum vitae.

People knew it and even expected it. In effect, even if the scribes who wrote the stories of the birth in Matthew and Luke were aware of the mistranslation of that word "almah", it was a very convenient mistake and one that could quite readily be left to carry a more powerful message.

Christian apologists often argue that the virgin birth stories of some of the ancient saviours are without any firm foundation, based on the historical evidence to hand.

To some degree, they are absolutely correct but equally it should be remembered that so many of the life stories of the deities seem to change depending on where they find a home. Different cultures had a different slant on the same myth. However, it is essential to bear in mind that the general motif of a supernatural birth always contained the concept of a mortal mother, sometimes a godly mother, and a superhuman father figure.

The need for the belief of the virgin birth of Jesus is essential to maintain a belief in the idea of Christ's deity as perceived by nearly all Christians today.

Any doubts about the validity of the birth story raises serious questions and when the followers of the old Mediterranean mystery cults accused the developing church of stealing their basic beliefs and adding a Christian slant to it, then the leaders like Irenaeus and Origen and Tertullian and Justin Martyr, had to dig deep to find answers.

The virgin birth is an underlying assumption of everything the Bible says about Jesus. To throw out the virgin birth is to reject Christ's deity, the accuracy and authority of scripture and a host of other related doctrines that are the heart of the Christian faith. No issue is more important than the virgin birth to our understanding of who Jesus is. If we deny Jesus is God, we have denied the very essence of Christianity. (John F. MacArthur Jr., R.C. Girard and Larry Richards, *The Life of Christ*, Thomas Nelson Publishers, 2007)

"The day will come when the mystical generation of Jesus by the Supreme Being as his father, in the womb of a virgin, will be classed with the fable of the generation of Minerva in the brain of Jupiter" (Thomas Jefferson, 1823).

"The awesomely influential nativity story in the first book of the New Testament is a speculative, rather than historical text. Far from being a report of a literal happening, it is an amalgam of flawed Greek – Christian scriptural references and of 'birth tales' current in Judaism in the first century AD. The story with which we are all so familiar is not fact but folklore" (Professor Geza Vermes, *The Authentic Gospel of Jesus*, Penguin 2004, Professor of Jewish Studies at Oxford University, retired 1991).

"To believe in a Christian way, you don't necessarily have to have a belief that literally Jesus was born from literally a virgin mother" (Dr David Jenkins. Ex Bishop of Durham, *The Independent on Sunday*, 5 February, 1994).

It was the great Philosopher Celsus, (writing circa 170 CE), who said,

Many of the nations of the world hold doctrines like those espoused by the Christians: The Galactophagi of Homer, the Druids of Gaul, and even the Getae believe doctrines very close to the historicity of Christianity and Judaism... Linus, Musaeus, Orpheus, Pherecydes, Zoroaster the Persian, and Pythagoras understood these doctrines. Clearly, the Christians have used the myths of the Danae and Melanippe, or of the Auge and the Antiope in fabricating the story of Jesus' virgin birth.

I think they may have a good point. When a scholar with the reputation of Geza Vermes says something as profound, and to most Christians as earth shattering as that, then very serious holes in the story are beginning to appear.

His comment about birth tales current in Judaism in the first century CE is very significant. Yet there are still many who claim that the nativity story was not influenced by the miraculous stories of Osiris, Dionysus, Mithras, Perseus, and Persephone, and even Origen mentions the virgin births of Danae, Melanippe, Auge and Antiope!

"The stories about these Gods are ancient but unlike the story of Jesus' virgin birth, only fables" (Origen, *Contra Celsum, 1*).

The Hellenistic virgin motif even gave rise to miraculous birth stories relating to human leaders of the day, like Alexander the Great and the Emperor Augustus, who were both regarded as deities.

It is quite easy to see where the title Son of God comes from; there were simply so many of them around.

Although the Bible does not mention a birth date for Jesus, it was not long before the bishops readily accepted 25 December as the recognized date.

It's no coincidence that so many of the mystery godmen share the same day.

This time of year was highly significant to the ancient

civilizations, who knew the importance of the time of the Winter Solstice in the underlying astrological beliefs within their mythology. This is a truly incredible part of the story and is something I will pursue a little later.

As we examine all of these pre-Christian similarities in the religions that predated the orthodox Church by, in some cases, thousands of years, we should bear in mind at all times, that none of the Jesus historical details, as known today, were ever mentioned in the very earliest scriptures that predated the gospels, which gave us an indication of time or place. In none of the early first-century writings do we hear anything about the details of a Jesus birth, life or death.

Many of the early scriptural texts such as the Letter of Barnabas, like so many others, do not mention a Mary or a Joseph, a Pontius Pilate, or the trial. No detail to give a clear historical outline. So, while the new religion of Christianity was developing in those early years, was the ever-present story of the miraculously born, resurrecting saviour figure, influencing the writers of the gospels, who had a myriad of myths and literature from all over the empire at their disposal? Yes, I believe so. The mystery religions were slowly making their mark on the Christian origins.

It is hard not to recognize the elements of what was known to the people of a thousand years before, when the birth story of Jesus Christ was created.

Almost every detail predates the Bible story. Even a birth in a stable is a reflection of the godmen of the Mysteries, who were often said to have been born in a cave. This cave idea dates to the dawn of time when mankind revering the sun as their god would assume the sun had retired to an underground cavern at the end of the day, where it fought its eternal battle with the power of darkness, only to win the day and reappear the next morning.

It would be unfair to Christian believers to say that the

early church simply stole all the ingredients of the Mystery Religions and made them their own. It did not happen like that. Christianity was a social product of its time and place. It did not invent its core concepts of heaven, hell, souls, eternal life, miracles, prophecies, angels, Gods, sons of God, walking, talking godmen, it got them from the culture in which it developed. When ancient people made a new religion, these are the things they put in.

Let us not forget the Magi, those wise men so well known to schoolchildren from their Christmas nativity play. The wise men, sometimes referred to as the Kings, were most likely mystical astrologers associated with the cult of Zoroaster and Mithra, a very ancient mystery religion originating in Persia. This fact would have been well known to the writer of the Gospel of Matthew, the only New Testament writer to mention them.

In Matthew's story, the wise men brought gifts of great value at the time of the birth of the Saviour, and this would carry the message to the early Christians as to just how important the child was perceived as being.

Equally, the Magi, as followers of the God Mithras and originally, the great Prophet Zoroaster, would have proven to the worshippers of the pagan gods that the birth of Jesus was such a major event, that even the mystics of the competing religions had followed a star to his birthplace to celebrate it.

In effect, the Jesus Christ religion was a continuation of the story originally attributed to the vegetative god stories of the distant past and adjusted to fit the needs of the Church at the time.

In that respect, just about all of the ingredients contained within the gospels have some parallels with the many, many philosophies of the time, which gave rise to the Mystery Religions and others from much further afield.

You would think that Matthew's story of Herod and the

massacre of the innocent children of Bethlehem would have made some impression on the historical writers of the day. Not a word of confirmation from any other source is offered to back up the heinous crime perpetrated by the much-loathed tyrant. Not even a reference from the first-century historian Josephus (38–107 CE), who wrote tirelessly about the man he despised.

There was no mention because it probably never happened. Again, it was part of the general motif abroad at the time.

The trade routes of India and Alexandria had resulted in a mixing of cultures adding even more to the belief patterns that could be shared and altered to fit the needs of any developing faith, just like Christianity. So, as in other elements of the Jesus story, the "massacre" theme had its roots elsewhere.

Even the Old Testament tells the story of the massacre of the children in Egypt and the scholar Albrecht Weber writes in his work, *Uber die Krishnajanmashtami,*

> Take, for example, the statement of the Vishnu Purana that Nanda, the foster father of Krishna, at the time of the latter's birth, went with his pregnant wife Yashoda to Mathura to pay taxes, or the pictorial representation of the birth of Krishna in the cowstall or shepherd's hut, that corresponds to the manger, and of the shepherds, shepherdesses, the ox and the ass that stand round the woman as she sleeps peacefully on her couch without fear or danger. Then the stories of the persecutions of Kamsa, of the massacre of the innocents.
> (Albrecht Weber, *Uber die Krishnajanmashtami*, Kessinger Publishing, 2010)

When you look at this, you must ask yourself who was influencing who when the myths were being invented? Considering that the stories of Krishna predate the gospel accounts by many centuries, it is certain that the Hindu and Buddhist influence was very evident at the end of the first century.

To stress the point, yet again, all the philosophies of the day were dipping into the pool of commonality, borrowing ideas and themes that were known and understood and developing them for a mythological creation of a new God, and yes, it is true that Christianity, as part of this theological mix, made its mark on other religions.

The mystery religion of Mithra is suggested by some scholars to have used some of the Christian motifs, as Mithraism grew to be a religion that posed huge problems for the early bishops.

The many ingredients of the life story of the Christian Messiah had developed just like all those other super gods because of syncretism of the sort of things that myth creators would use in those distant days.

We have already looked at some of the obvious storylines that appear in one form or another elsewhere, but what about the miracles of Jesus Christ, surely they were unique, a one-off divinely inspired ability to make the impossible possible.

Well, no, they all did it. The miracle stories abounded at the time and related not only to the godmen but even to the deified humans like the Roman emperors who were so godlike that one supposedly restored the sight of a blind man by using his spittle, rubbed on the unfortunate's eyes.

Miracles and magical tricks were part of the culture at the time. It is what they did and what they believed, and it was not unusual.

Followers of the mystery godman Dionysus, originally a god of wine and known to the faithful in Rome as Bacchus, was believed to have turned water into wine. The story had some variations, one of which included a stream of water turning to wine via his miracle and another where the stream of wine flowing in his temple would turn to water when taken away.

Bacchus, too, was responsible for causing empty vessels to fill with wine when sealed in a locked room. Truly miraculous!

The comparison with the miraculous deeds of the Messiah

of the Christians is too obvious to mention! Remember the wedding at Cana? Jesus was being made to show he could do it better. He was in fact, "the true vine".

Travelling wonder workers were common at the time of Matthew, Mark, Luke and John's hagiographies and they were aware of most or all of the stories and travelling mystics who were responsible for them.

Once upon a time, there was a man called Asclepius, (sometimes Asclepios), who was a son of God, and was renowned for his medical skills. So famous did he become, that a cult developed around him and his miraculous works. He cured madness by casting out demons, he cured the sick and he raised people from the dead. This did not go down too well with the rulers of the Underworld who thought they were being cheated out of a few candidates.

As a result, Hades, the shady God of downstairs, had a word with the super god Zeus, who blasted the innocent Asclepius with a thunderbolt, killing him stone dead!

Fortunately, as is the case with most of these meaningful mythical tales, there is a happy ending. Our hero is resurrected by his dad, Apollo, and he lives happily ever after.

The cult of Asclepius had an alarming effect on the early Church, the similarities of the earlier pagan wonder workers were difficult to refute.

The similarity between the deeds of Christ and of Asclepius is in many respects striking and it was "the similarity between the deeds of Christ and of Asclepius that was bound to heighten the controversy between the Christian faith and the Asclepius religion" (Edelstein, *Asclepius II*, p. 133).

For the simple folk of the time, both Jesus and Asclepius could have been interchangeable. They were both considered Saviours and readily associated themselves with poor and oppressed people. They were regular miracle workers and healed the sick, for which they claimed no payment.

The pagan god was a serious contender for the position of top miracle worker and there were as many attested miracles attributed to our resurrected pagan god as there were to the Christian Saviour, Jesus.

Did they do what was the usual thing of the day and create a few similar anecdotes to the Asclepius accounts that were known to men and women in the street as common knowledge? Were the accounts of Jesus' wonder workings a genuine, one-off description of something unique and miraculous that had not been witnessed before?

The evidence would not appear to support this. Again, we see the same motif expressed in different ways but then again, we do see parallel miracles such as raising the dead.

Without any knowledge of any of the associated subjects of the Mystery Religions, Hellenistic philosophy, ancient history the background to the origins of the gospels, it's easy to see how the story we were taught at school became, for most of us, the unique revelation of the true Saviour that it ultimately became; never doubted, never questioned.

As the world of ancient knowledge opened before me, as I progressed on my personal journey of searching out the facts behind the historicity of the Jesus Christ godman, I was stunned to see how relevant the myths of deities like Asclepius were, in putting some perspective into the Jesus "truths" and it forced me to look at, literally, everything in the Old and New Testaments in a different light.

Without an insight into the life and works, albeit mythical, of the Asclepius character, I would never have been able to view the miraculous tales of the New Testament with the somewhat cynical eye, which I now do.

Miracles were important to the gospel writers. Jesus had to be seen to be able to keep up with all those other practitioners of supernatural deeds.

There were very many of these travelling magicians on the

streets of Judea and Alexandria in the first century CE and one that ought to be mentioned when looking at the Jesus similarities, is the travelling wonder worker known as Apollonius of Tyana. We know only a little about this Greek Neopythagorean philosopher but what we do, comes from the pen of Philostratus the Elder (circa 170 247 CE), who in his biography of the orator, places him around the time of 15–98 CE.

So great was the fame of our miracle man at the time, that the much-quoted Church historian Eusebius says that he was compared to Jesus Christ by Christians in the fourth century (Eusebius 260–340 CE).

Philostratus, in his biography *Life of Apollonius of Tyana*, points out his many miracle deeds and it becomes ever more obvious just how similarly, again, this miracle worker reflected the miracle worker from Nazareth.

Porphyry, an anti-Christian Neoplatonist claimed in his *Against the Christians*, that none of the works of Jesus could be considered unique and mentioned Apollonius as a non-Christian who shared similar achievements.

Heracles, in about 303 CE, argued that the great man Apollonius had exceeded the works of Jesus yet still did not receive a God status and that the cultured biographers of the sage were more trustworthy than the uneducated apostles of the competing Jesus.

Apollonius was said to have travelled and worked his magic around Antioch, Ephesus, Cilicia and Byzantium and there is evidence of there having been a shrine to him at Tyana.

The similarities between Jesus and Apollonius of Tyana are significant and don't warrant scornful dismissal. Although both men came from different religious, economic, and social backgrounds, the fact of such startling similarities in how they came to be conceptualised as divine mediator figures cannot be put down to coincidence or conceptual plagiarism. Since both men were contemporaneous with one another, it is likely that the ways in which both figures came to be perceived, was consistent with an underlying subconscious schema embedded within the first century East Mediterranean mindset.

The quest for the historical Jesus should not neglect to compare and contrast Jesus and his traditions with the enigmatic and fascinating figure of Apollonius of Tyana.

(Andrew G. Home-Cook, *Apollonius of Tyana as a divine Mediator*, University of St Andrews School of Divinity, 1998)

So, there lies another problem to take on board when looking at the veracity of the miracle stories supposedly perpetrated by the personification of the spiritual being brought to us originally in a vision experienced by Paul the Evangelist.

As the reader of our journey into history, I do not know just how much, or how little, knowledge you had of all these extraneous elements to the basic story but I think you will agree that it is hard to deny that an understanding of the biblical "truth" cannot be possible without some profound understanding of these other things. Remember throughout, that these are the same extraneous elements that Christian apologists will totally ignore and confirm their historical validity via blind faith alone.

We have made the point that so much of the commonly understood and believed content has its roots elsewhere, and we know just how important the idea of a virgin birth and miracles and resurrection has on the "uniqueness" of the faith. Well, maybe several other aspects of that faith should be looked at to see just how unique that faith really is.

In my early reading, the doubts and grave doubts at that, about the miraculous birth really did alter my whole concept of the religion as a whole.

I knew little or nothing of the rites and the belief patterns of the very many mystery religions but what I had gleaned had already planted the seeds of doubt.

Take baptism, for example. Did you, like me, think that this was something instigated by the one and only John the Baptist in the Gospel of Mark? It was apparently an important part of the story because it is the start of the whole Christian story according to the gospels. The Gospel of Mark was written first and there was no birth episode in this gospel, so the rites of baptism were obviously very important.

Is this another case of the ancients having got there first? The mystery religions predated the Christians by centuries with the use of baptism as a cleansing rite of purification and initiation.

The church father Tertullian (circa 160–220 CE) said, "In certain mysteries, it is by baptism that members are initiated."

Justin Martyr the great defender of the faith (100–165 CE) once again blamed yet another similarity in the Christian belief as something that the demons and devils had learned from the Book of Isaiah and taught it to the followers of the Mysteries.

The Bible tells us that John the Baptist would baptize people into the faith in the River Jordan, where at the same time they would confess their sins.

Plutarch (46–125 CE) philosopher and Priest of Apollo at Delphi, tells us,

"When Antalcidas was being initiated into the mysteries at Samothrace, he was asked by the priest to confess what especially dreadful thing he had done during his life" (*The Origins of Christianity and the Bible*, Andrew Benson, Prudential Pub Co; Revised edition, 2000).

Historically, it would seem likely that the early Christians maintained the ceremony of baptism and cleansing from a far earlier cult and that rite was adopted by John the Baptist, who was not a Christian. Christians still had not been invented at the time of his wanderings in the wilderness, eating locusts and wild honey.

The Jewish sect that the Baptist came from obviously was

associated with baptism, that is complete immersion and purification of the soul.

Judaism did not involve itself with that sort of thing, but the Essene sect did and it was this Jewish sect that we think John the Baptist belonged to. The Essenes were an incredibly important sect of the Jewish people that played a major part in the origins of Christianity, and we will be looking closer at their history later.

As John the Baptist plays such an important role in the Gospel of Mark, it would seem more than likely that the Christian originators borrowed this practice directly from him and his Jewish sect, the Essenes, who in turn had inherited it, along with many other philosophies from the practitioners of the many mystery cults in existence, centuries before the turn of the era.

Not being a Christian, it is interesting to know what the Baptist initiated people into?

Mark tells us that it was not in the name of Jesus Christ.

Andrew Benson puts it quite succinctly when he writes,

Christianity was a continuation of pre-existing beliefs. As we will further examine, it was created by the fusion or syncretism of Judaic and Greek beliefs. Such syncretism was common during that era. Religions were put together using elements of other religions. All mystery religions shared common beliefs. People were not offended by such inter borrowing. The mystery religions were not competing with one another. They got along harmoniously. People belonged to several mystery religions simultaneously. Only Christianity prohibited its converts from belonging to other religions. This was not a problem in the beginning. However, when Christians grew in numbers in the second century CE, the other religions became offended by Christianity's competitiveness and its lack of sharing.

(*The Origins of Christianity and the Bible,* Andrew Benson, Prudential Pub Co; Revised edition, 2000)

Baptism is a pagan ritual and certainly appears to have been taken on board by the Christian fathers. Learning more about the ceremony from the other mystery religions gives a further insight into other elements of the Jesus story.

For instance, we have already mentioned the ancient cult of Mithraism, a religion, which competed in popularity with Christianity for the first few centuries of the Common Era.

Shrines to the mystery god Mithras are found all over the empire, several of which are in Britain and we know from the historian Plutarch that the religion was practised in parts of the Mediterranean as early as 67 BCE.

The popularity of the cult was noted by many of the early historians and we read accounts from the Philosopher Porphyry (232–303 CE) and the early Christian scholar Origen, and of course St Jerome, who had a lot to say about things that didn't fit into his philosophy.

As in so many of the Mediterranean cults, this too had astonishing similarities to the early cult of the Christians. There was a rite of baptism involving immersion as a way of purification or by sprinkling with their holy water. At this initiation, honey would be spread on the hands and the tongue of the celebrant and as Porphyry explained, it was believed that honey was a powerful preservative and would thus keep the initiate free from sin.

The temple to Mithras was called the Mithraeum, a cave-like room, where the representation of Mithras killing the sacred bull, the Tauroctony, would be found.

The bull is thought to have had its origins in astrological symbolism and did not refer to actual animal sacrifice, simply as a sacrifice, however, spilling of the animal's blood was an essential part of the initiation.

It was here that the celebrant would enter a pit and above him, a bull would be slaughtered, baptising the initiate in the blood of the slaughtered animal.

A bit of a contradiction but the representation of the slaying by Mithras is almost certainly an astrological depiction of the end of the Age of Taurus, but this is debated by some scholars.

You may be surprised, but by now probably not, to learn that St Peter's Basilica in Rome stands on the spot on which the last Taurobolium, the blood baptism of the bull slaughter, took place in the fourth century CE (David Fingrut, "Essay on Mithraism: The Legacy of the Roman Empire's Final State Religion", 1993).

The blood of animals like bulls, rams and goats is quite well known in the rites of baptism and the expression "washed in the blood of the lamb" is evidently based on these ceremonies, and of course, Christianity would have had its own astrological significance in the "death of the ram", as Jesus marked the dawning of the Age of Pisces after the Age of Aries.

Whether it was by immersion in the sea, such as at the Eleusinian Mystery or immersion in a pool or by drenching in blood, it seems that very many of the religions practised at the time of the gospel writing, saw baptism as a vital ingredient in the ceremony of initiation and in the Gospel of Mark, it is the very first thing we read about at the arrival of the Chosen One.

Do not forget, Mark is the first of the gospels, not Matthew, as it appears in the New Testament. It was obviously a very important part of the story, because as we have already pointed out, there is no birth narrative in Mark.

The dove that descends from above at the time of baptism by John the Baptist and the spooky voice from the heavens that accompanies it, is the way that, for Mark, Jesus was given his badge of total holiness.

The early Christians knew how important baptism was to the followers of the various mystery religions at the time, so it would be an obvious advantage to use the ceremony in their fledgling faith too, if it was to attract followers from the pagan faiths.

The great Church fathers, like the ever present, Irenaeus,

Justin Martyr, Origen and Tertullian, all had an uphill struggle to find convincing answers to the criticism hurled against them about Christianity not displaying anything particularly, new compared to the much older mystery religions that the people of the time found perfectly adequate for their spiritual needs.

It is hard to argue that the syncretism of religious motifs had not been absorbed by the gospel compilers, just like the philosophers of more ancient times had done with their allegorical, and deeply spiritual, myths about the many Gods revered around the lands of the Mediterranean.

The only defence that the early bishops could come up with was that the Devil had planted all of these "truths" from the Jesus story into those many older religions as a pre-emptive strike against the Jesus story, so that their Gods could claim what the Christian Saviour would do later!

This has become known as Diabolical Mimicry and Justin Martyr was a master at calling on it when he thought he had a problem!

> by the influence of the wicked demons, to deceive and lead astray the human race. For having heard it proclaimed through the prophets that the Christ was to come and that the ungodly among men were to be punished by fire, they put forward many to be called sons of Jupiter, under the impression that they would be able to produce in men the idea that the things which were said with regard to Christ, were mere marvellous tales, like the things which were said by the poets.
>
> (Justin Martyr, *First Apology*)

They simply could not accept that the promises offered by the other religions could be anything like what was on offer to the followers of the one true faith. We accept without question the claims of the Bible stories because that is what we have always known. We find it a bit silly to even consider the stories of those backward pagan people to have any substance whatsoever, after all they're only fairy stories, are they not?

We do not accept any of their claims because we know absolutely nothing about them. Most of us have never heard of Mithras, Dionysus, Osiris, and the rest, and we certainly do not understand the highly complicated philosophy and spiritual path that the myths are founded on. If we don't understand it, it simply doesn't exist. Therefore, the Jesus miracles and the life and death reports are factual, because they are the word of God. The pagan myths are only for children.

It must be ever more obvious that the Christ stories are allegorical, just like the ancient myths and that is probably why the content is very similar. We have found similarities, occasionally identical, in both the gospels and the stories of the mystery godmen.

If we dig a little deeper, even more of the content of the New Testament reports seem to have their roots in another place and time. Take the Eucharist, another major ingredient in the ceremonial procedures of the early and present-day Church.

The Eucharist, also called the Holy Communion, the Blessed Sacrament, or the Lord's Supper, is looked upon as a re-enactment of the final meal, the Last Supper, that Jesus shared with his disciples, before the crucifixion.

He gave them bread saying, "This is my body," and wine saying, "this is my blood."

Really emotive words that have resonated with the faithful over two thousand years.

It is even mentioned as early as one of the Letters of Paul, which we referred to earlier,

"the Lord Jesus the same night in which he was betrayed took bread: And when he had given thanks, he brake it, and said, Take, eat: this is my body, which is broken for you: this do in remembrance of me" (1 Corinthians, 11:23, 24).

We have mentioned earlier that Paul relates to something that for once might just be an historical account of something that Jesus said and did, which is, as we know, glaringly absent in the Letters of Paul.

Well again, there is nothing new or unique about this ceremony. Paul was very aware of the diverse religious cultures of the day, which had been involved in similar rites for centuries, before the Christians adopted the same.

The old religions, like Christianity, perceived the special presence of their Christ during the communal ceremony of transubstantiation.

The noted historians the Durants point out that it is, "one of the oldest ceremonies of primitive religion" (W. and A. Durant, *The Story of Civilization,* Simon and Schuster, 1975).

The priests of ancient Egypt would use small baked cakes which they believed would turn into the flesh of their saviour, Osiris, and even the peoples of South America were using an identical rite, when they used flour and water to create an image of their deity, which they ate, something that astonished the Spanish missionaries when they witnessed it as it was all a bit familiar (Prescott's Mexico Vol. 3. as related by Bartholomew F. Brewer PhD. in *The Mystery of the Eucharist*).

For the ancient practitioners of the rite, it was never meant to be a literal transformation of wine to blood and bread to body, it was meant only in a mystical sense. The celebrant shared the divine vitality with the deity.

"The Dionysian Mysteries had a communion, in which the priests and the congregation together partook of the blood and of the flesh of the divinity Dionysus. The blood was wine, the flesh was cereal, bread if you wish, or wheat" (*Studies in Occult Philosophy,* G. de Purucker, Theosophical University Press, 1973).

Many of the ancient gods were associated with the concept of corn, grain bread, and wine, which is an echo of their origins as agricultural deities.

Osiris is killed and his body torn apart and scattered, symbolizing the threshing of the corn to make bread.

Other mystery godmen have stories in their myths, which are all so similar, and even Jesus relates to himself as the true vine.

Hopefully, you like me, will now be starting to realize that so much of the mythological detail, buried within the ancient texts, had an inner, more spiritual meaning, than what the outer meaning of the myth would, at first, have you believe.

The ceremony of the bread and wine was yet another of the allegorical elements, concealed within the mysteries, it was never meant to be taken as a literal miracle.

As long ago as when Cicero was writing his work *The Nature of the Gods* circa 60 BCE, he realized the allegorical nature of the Eucharist, when he says, "is anybody so mad as to believe that the food which he eats is actually a god?"

I suggest that the borrowing of the various motifs across the boundaries of the mystery religions and ultimately into the pages of the New Testament, is something that most Christians will simply have to accept. Apologists make numerous claims to deny the obvious but we, having only looked at the miraculous birth, the baptism, the miracles, and the Holy Communion, already can make a good case for the idea of the sharing of the general motif from very ancient times, that so many scholars now perceive as being the foundations of the Christian story.

To satisfy the critics and the apologists, I will reaffirm that no one god or religion predating the Christian account, mirrors Jesus or his life exactly. I do not know of anybody who makes this claim, but the elements from the whole spectrum of Egyptian, Greek and Persian belief patterns, not to mention the Buddhist influence, are so very evident.

The death of the godman and his return to life, is the central tenet for the followers of all the mystery religions and certainly for the faithful adherents of the modern church.

A belief in the virgin birth, the crucifixion, and the resurrection of the flesh, are without doubt, the most important themes in the faith. Without these ingredients, the Christian religion would have no foundation whatsoever.

You may remember, at the outset, we identified a very real, very successful brand of Christianity, developed by the spiritual, philosophical, mystical thinkers, called the Gnostics, who did not believe any of that sort of thing. To them, the orthodox Christians were the heretics.

It certainly seems that the death and resurrection of Jesus Christ is yet another allegorical theme. Let us have a closer look in the next chapter.

Chapter 5

The Righteous Man; His Crucifixion and Resurrection

The ancient origins of the resurrection motif undoubtedly developed from the very early agricultural necessities of a vegetative based deity. One who would keep the land fertile, give up his life for his followers and reappear again to continue the cycle for ever.

Dionysus, or Bacchus in his other guise, reflects the tragic story of the death and rebirth of vegetation and as Frazer indicates in *The Golden Bough,* the tale reappears in the Myths of Demeter and Persephone, Aphrodite and Adonis, Cybele and Attis and the classic story of Isis and Osiris.

"A goddess mourns the loss of a loved one, who personifies the vegetation (corn), which dies in winter to revive in Spring" (*The Golden Bough: A Study in Religion and Magic*, Sir James George Frazer, Dover Publications Inc. 2003).

The gospels' account of Jesus being hauled before Pontius Pilate and questioned about his Divinity and his alleged crimes, are well known. A simple, innocent, easy going guy, condemned for doing something on charges that don't seem to have much foundation, is a scenario found elsewhere, outside of the gospel story.

The Mysteries were using this tearjerker centuries before the church founders were able to relate to it.

Euripides, (484–407 BCE), was a writer of Greek tragedies and composed the famous work about Dionysus *The Bacchae* in which he tells the tale of our hero Dionysus being brought before the not very nice ruler King Pentheus, and has to answer charges relating to his claims of divinity and other dubious accusations.

Like Jesus, he gives as good as he gets and like Jesus, too, he promises all sorts of godly revenge as he is taken away by the boys in blue.

All of this and so much more, was being fed to the followers of the Mysteries, certainly four hundred years before the Christians took up the theme.

It does look a bit similar doesn't it?

The obvious parallel with Christianity is observed by Barry B. Powell in his work *Classical Myth*, Second Edition, Pearson College Div; 1997, in which he also comments on the parallels to be found in the bread and wine ritual and the notion of transubstantiation that can be found in the much earlier religion of Dionysus.

The hero god figures, like Jesus, are taken away to their fate, innocent and righteous, they accept their fate in a matter-of-fact sort of way!

Even the earthbound philosophers, who were not deities in the eyes of the common man, were known for their cool acceptance of their fate after being found guilty on suspicious charges.

In their incredibly comprehensive study of the pagan origins of Christianity titled *The Jesus Mysteries: Was The 'Original Jesus' A Pagan God?*, Thorsons, 1999, Timothy Freke and Peter Gandy mention the story of Socrates, who like Jesus, a righteous man, was condemned to death for his heresies. Socrates accepted his fate without question and before his death his friends offered to pay thirty pieces of silver on his behalf to free him. Socrates was having none of it. It was a betrayal of his desire to remain true to his principles.

Does thirty pieces of silver ring any bells?

The righteous good guy suffering at the hands of the corrupt sheriff was a familiar ingredient in the ancient dramas and even Plato the Pythagorean philosopher, (429–348 BCE) talks about testing the just or righteous man to see if he is truly "just and righteous".

[T]he only way to test righteousness is to give this man every injustice the world can inflict.

What they will say is this: that such being his disposition the just man will have to endure the lash, the rack, the chains, the branding iron in his eyes and finally after every extremity of suffering, he will be crucified and so will learn his lesson that not to be but to seem just is what we ought to desire. (Plato, *Republic*, 2.361e)

When Plato uses the word crucify, he uses the Greek word *anaskolopizo* which means to fix on a pole or a stake or to impale.

Plato had a lot to say about the ever present "just" man and the all-suffering "righteous " man. Do you think the Jesus Christ biographers knew about any of this? Of course, they did! Not only was the work of Plato renowned amongst the educated at the end of the first century CE, but the general motif of a badly treated good guy, was a common theme in the myths of the time. It was Celsus, that arch critic of Christianity, writing in the mid second century CE, who never missed an opportunity to berate the developing Church for copying every pagan myth, and who criticised the church fathers for saying that their story of the righteous man was unique.

Having been found guilty as charged and taken away to be crucified in the manner so graphically described in the gospels, it is this tragic, cruel loss that has left its mark on the soul of every committed Christian who recognizes this sacrifice as the means of salvation for mankind. They believe Jesus truly died an horrendous death on the cross to pay for the sins of us all.

It is often mentioned in many of the works of scholars and pseudo scholars, that the mystery godmen met their fate in a similar way to that of the Christian Messiah: just another dip into that pool of common elements. Well, this time this does not seem to be the case, or as commonplace as they would have us believe.

It does all get a bit complicated, because as we established earlier not all the myths relating to our mythical god figures have the same life stories. The stories change, but the motif remains as the myth is adopted in different parts of the lands in which it is practised.

We know from textual and archaeological evidence that the mystery godmen, including Dionysus, Osiris, Attis, Mithras and all those that represent the same mythical entity in different guises, gave their lives for the good of the people in a truly cruel way. There are undoubtedly some representations on vases depicting Dionysus and a cross, but it seems Jesus has the copyright on a crucifixion as we know it.

But wait a moment. Was Jesus crucified in the manner that we accept as a universal truth? When I was studying the Letters of Paul, many years ago, it confused me enormously to read in Galatians 3:13:

"Christ redeemed us from the curse of the law by becoming a curse for us – for it is written, 'cursed is everyone who hangs on a tree', in order that in Christ Jesus, the blessings of Abraham might come to the Gentiles, so that we might receive the promise of the spirit through faith."

Hangs on a tree? I read on and in Acts 5:30, I was astonished to read, "The God of our ancestors raised up Jesus, whom you had killed by hanging Him on a tree."

In Acts 10:39, we read, "They put Him to death by hanging Him on a tree."

It is there, really. Have a look! So, what's with this tree hanging business? I'm sure a very scholarly Doctor of Divinity could provide me with an erudite answer but I'm sure too, that the same worthy Doctor would ignore some of the death stories that relate to our superheroes and their associations with trees.

One of the many saviours we have mentioned is the godman Attis. He was born as a Son of God, considered to have been slain for the salvation of his followers, bread was eaten to represent his body, in some cultures they celebrated his birthday on 25 December and he came back to life after three days.

All the usual stuff is there but it's interesting to note that his death is described sometimes as being caused by castration under a tree, where his blood flowed and redeemed the earth for his people.

His death and rebirth were celebrated on 25 March and he was believed to be reborn as an evergreen pine tree and sometimes revived to life by Cybele.

The festival to celebrate his life and death involved a figure of the godman who had been hung on the tree and was left for three days in a cave tomb, where after the three days, he was reborn.

The myth of Attis was hugely popular and the tree motif would be widely known to the gospel writers.

On the other hand, a deeper look at the concept of crucifixion as far as the Jews were concerned, opens up a whole new array of possibilities.

The highly respected Israeli archaeologist Yigael Yadin (1917–1984) has shown from his work on the Temple Scroll, part of the ancient Dead Sea Scrolls, that from the early second century BCE to the fall of the temple in 70 CE, some Jewish sects held that anyone guilty of treason or blasphemy, should die by being hanged upon a tree, and while he is hanging on the tree, he is, according to the Torah, "accursed by God and men".

It was the Essenes and the Sadducees who held this view and, of course, it was the Sadducees who were the priests of the Temple in the time of Jesus.

They were the leaders outraged by Jesus' claims and accused him of speaking blasphemy and as such, called for the punishment of hanging from a tree. In the gospel, Jesus certainly poses a threat to the leadership of the Temple and they called for the law to be implemented and to hang him on a tree, which only Pontius Pilate could implement.

Interestingly, it was this call for the death of Jesus that led to nearly two thousand years of anti-Semitism; blaming the Jewish nation for the death of the Christian Messiah.

If it ever did happen at all, it was the small group of Temple leaders and the Roman rulers who were responsible; the persecution of the Jewish people, as a result, has been an absolute travesty.

Remember too, the very early Church would have been only too pleased to go along with this accusation, as it demonstrated to the Romans that they were very different to those Jews, whom the Romans were always a bit suspicious of. They could not tell the difference, most of the time, between the Jews and the Christians.

The theology behind the crucifixion and the meaning of it and the symbolism and the type of cross, if a cross was used at all, and so on, has taxed the minds of biblical scholars for centuries.

It is not as clear cut as the Bible would have you believe. The image of the just man, badly treated, on the traditional cross, dying a horrible death for us is certainly a powerful image and one which has carried the ultimate message of Christianity to the present day.

Debates between scholars still rage over so many elements of the story. Some suggest that the crucifixion as we know it, that is hung on a Roman cross, is a fiction and was not added to the story until 67 CE. Many cite that the biblical Peter, who was meant to have been an eyewitness to the crucifixion according to the New Testament, is the very one who tells us that Jesus was hanged on a tree.

And so, it gets ever more complicated. Does it really matter? Yes, it certainly does because it proves the point, if any more proof was needed, that "The things that you're liable, to read in the Bible, it ain't necessarily so."

There is so much more going on in the pages of the New testament than what you get from reading the stories as literal accounts of a miraculous superhero who stood head and shoulders above all those other "pagan" gods.

If even the crucifixion is not as clear cut an issue as we thought, then what is?

By studying the Greek words for cross, scholars have tried endlessly to come to some sort of agreement as to something as simple as the shape of that cross.

Was it a pole or a cross, similar to what your Aunt Rose wore around her neck? Or was it a T-shaped cross or a Tau, or indeed was it a tree? What does it matter? At the end of the day, it was the death of the man that really matters, is it not?

Well, I do not know how the faithful would react to the story if it was confirmed that Jesus did die in the manner of a convicted blasphemer and was hanged on a tree, and the traditional scene was indeed a later add on?

The cross in its various manifestations has been a symbol shared by virtually all the ancient religions and, in one way or another, many of those ancient godmen are shown in conjunction with the cross.

The very ancient cross of the Egyptians, called the Ankh, is easily recognized as the T-shaped cross with the loop above. It is evident on the walls of pyramids and is the old hieroglyph meaning life.

It is undoubtedly a phallic symbol, representing the male and female organs, the phallic aspect is true, too, of the well-known cross of the Christians.

Once again, we have a vital element of the Christian story, that is – the cross, which is highly symbolic in those other pagan religions, where it was revered as the "source of life". Have you noticed how the Ankh looks like a person with outstretched arms?

In summary, to say that the crucifixion claim about the godman of Christianity is unique is not correct. There are other references we can allude to that show similarities in other myths.

Parallels are drawn between the Christian story and much

earlier mythology by respected historian Richard Carrier who says,

> The only case I know of a pre-Christian God actually being crucified and then resurrected is Inanna (also known as Ishtar), a Sumerian goddess, whose crucifixion, resurrection and escape from the underworld is told in cuneiform tablets inscribed in circa 1500 BC, attesting to a very old tradition... (Richard Carrier, From an essay regarding the work of Kersey Graves and his book, *The World's Sixteen Crucified Saviours*, Book Tree, 1999).

He also mentions the story of Zalmoxis, (described in the mid fifth century BCE by Herodotus), who is the only pre-Christian man to be buried and resurrected and deified in his own lifetime.

The "resurrection" was not quite the miracle it appeared to be, but as a result, a religion surrounding him, promising heavenly immortality, continued for centuries.

The death of the gods in all the myths, including the Christian account, are truly elaborate affairs and are coloured with some fantastic detail to give credibility to the initiate.

If you examine the Gospel of Matthew at chapter 27:50, you will be astonished to read something that most people are unaware of.

Here, it tells the story that at the time of Jesus' death on the cross, a remarkable event took place. Matthew tells us that the ground and tombs were split open, and the dead were raised and walked, quite casually, into the city, where no doubt, they met up with old friends and lived happily ever after! Maybe too, to die another natural death later?

Do you really believe this? Does any committed Christian believe this? Why was this incredible account of a crowd of zombies walking around town not reported by the articulate, educated historians of the day?

Not a word about this event at the time of the crucifixion has been recorded anywhere!

If Paul had known about this piece of "history", can you imagine the letter the Galatians would have received?

We all know that this is a bit of dressing up of the main theme: something to give it the wow factor. It certainly does that. Ask any church-going Christian about this myth and they will either be totally unaware of it, as most are, or squirm uncomfortably and reluctantly admit that it's probably a fib.

Why does this major element in the crucifixion account have less credibility than any other of the story's content? Is it simply because it's too outrageous to believe? If that is the case, I don't think it reflects well on the rest of the saga.

The one thing the Christians do have on their side relating to the dying and resurrecting motif is that he was, according to the gospel writers, a very real person. Unlike the gods of Mithras, Osiris, Dionysus *et al.* Jesus could claim to be real and as such, his life and death carried a lot more resonance.

He died the death that was expected for the righteous, just man that he was at his time.

Whereas the older gods of myth died a death in some ways representing the corn motif that they originally represented, like Osiris, torn apart, shredded, just like corn when making bread, Jesus died the horrible death of a real being in a way that they all knew.

It's worth mentioning here that the corn vegetative motif is, in a clever way, carried on by Jesus.

The Old Testament, as we have said, carries all the predictions of the gospel created Christ, including the fact that he had to be born in Bethlehem, and born in Bethlehem he was, according to Matthew and Luke. Ask any Hebrew speaker what the meaning of the word Bethlehem is and you will be amazed. It means "the house of bread"! This is not a coincidence. And not only that, but the figure depicting the virgin in the constellation of Virgo is always shown as holding stalks of grain. Mary in the house of bread.

The deaths of the mystery gods do, however, show remarkable similarities to some of the other well-known aspects of the death of Jesus or Yeshua, to use his correct name.

When Jesus is given the vinegar or gall to drink, as he dies on the cross, so too the priest at the mystery celebrations of Dionysus is given gall to drink when the celebrants drink wine.

The incredibly widespread religion of Mithras around the Empire often depicts their God in association with two torch bearers, one on either side of him. These are considered the celestial twins of light and darkness or maybe the two equinoxes. Some relate the twins to the brothers of ancient myth Castor and Pollux, and the same motif is found in the worship of Bacchus or Dionysus. This is to be compared with the two criminals crucified alongside Jesus: one is promised a trip to heaven whilst the other goes in the other direction to a not too certain future in the fire and brimstone.

The torch bearers of the mysteries are always depicted as having one torch pointing upwards and the other down, implying the Heaven and Hell concept.

Readers wishing to investigate the deeper meaning behind the apparently simple story of the two thieves sentenced to die with Jesus, will be astonished to discover just how deep and symbolic the story becomes, when the name of one of them, Jesus Barabbas is analysed for its deeper meaning, which is "son of the father". You can see how quickly that becomes a bit messy.

It should be noted, too, that the gospel tells the story of how it was tradition to release a prisoner at the time of Passover, one who the crowd would choose. As we know they chose Barabbas (Mark 15:6). There is no record anywhere of this custom ever having existed. It appears only in the gospels and none of the historians of the day, whose works still exist, ever relate to it.

The scholar Hyam Maccoby argues that when the crowd gathered before Pilate and chanted to free Bar Abba, they may well have meant Jesus, but anti-Semitic elements in the developing Church juggled things to make it look like the Jews were responsible for the crucifixion of the Christian Saviour, letting the Romans off quite lightly.

Of course, as with most of the whole narrative, we have evidence of something similar elsewhere.

Dennis R. MacDonald in his brilliant work *The Homeric Epics and the Gospel of Mark*, Yale University Press, 2010, notes that a very similar episode to that of the crowd picking one figure over another and very similar to the other, occurs in Homer's *Odyssey*, written centuries before the Gospels. He suggests that this highlights the cruelty of Jesus' persecutors.

You would think that something as stark as the crown of thorns would be unique but no, Dionysus was made to wear a crown of symbolic ivy, and as Freke and Gandy point out in *The Jesus Mysteries: Was The 'Original Jesus' a Pagan God?* Harmony, 2001.

"Just as Jesus is dressed up in purple robes when he is ridiculed by the Roman soldiers, so Dionysus was also dressed in purple robes and initiates at Eleusis wore a purple sash wrapped around their bodies."

It is clear to see that all the great gods of the time, Bacchus, Dionysus, Attis, Osiris, and of course, Jesus, who took his place amongst them, died a sacrificial death for his followers. It was symbolic and indeed it was expected. By taking part in the Passion, the followers of the mystery religions were able to undergo a spiritual rebirth and based on the eternal concept of ancient philosophy, shared by those early Christians we call the Gnostics, they were "born again" to a higher self. It was all allegorical symbolism.

Their sacrificial deaths were different and yet they were the same. They died in a manner of their time but all of them, one way or another, were destined to return to the joy of their faithful followers. Their deaths, described in so many ways, depending on the culture of those telling the tale, has its counterpart in the death of Jesus. Was he crucified on a Roman cross, a pole, or was he hanged in a tree, as we are told in several places in the Bible? Why do we have no pictorial depictions of a man on a cross until the fifth century CE?

The belief in the dying and "resurrecting" godman is a story that is as old as written history, or should that be mythology? And that coming back to life motif is so often associated with the Vernal Equinox, or as we call it Easter, the time that vegetation comes alive again and notably, the Sun, the earliest of all the gods, and with which so many pagan gods are associated, also, "resurrects" for the rest of the year.

It was near impossible for Justin Martyr, Tertullian, or any of the early defenders of Christianity, to make a good argument against the obvious syncretism that was taking place in all the religious cults of their time. It was clear to see that the dying and resurrecting Saviour of the orthodox church, was another in the long line of deities whose life story reflected so many of the well-known ingredients, that it made changing your allegiance between any of the mystery religions, or the new faith, quite a simple matter and of course, the rules of membership and the salvation promised by Christianity, made it a popular choice, especially as Celsus points out, for the ignorant and the uneducated.

Before we move on from this topic, I want to list the similarities that other religions would have shared at the time of the arrival of Jesus Christ, Saviour, Messiah, and Redeemer of mankind.

For those who still argue that no other mystery religion is a mirror image of the Christian story, I will repeat myself and say that the point is well made, but any one of the principal elements of the Gospels, has some pre-existence in another culture, whether that be the mystery religions, Buddhism or Hinduism. That word syncretism is most certainly making its presence felt:

The gods of ancient times were the sons of the mythical super-gods and were known as the Son of God, so too was Jesus.

All the pagan saviours claim a supernatural birth, or in many cases, a virgin birth. So too does Jesus.

Very many of the older saviours share 25 December as a birth date – the date of the rebirth of the Sun, so too does Jesus. (The Bible does not mention this date.)

Some of the birth stories of the earlier deities claim that shepherds and wise men were present at the time, so too does the Jesus story.

In some accounts of the ancient myth, as in the Osiris narrative, a star plays a major part in heralding the arrival of the Saviour. The star of Bethlehem is well known in the Jesus story.

Ritual cleansing of sins in water or baptism plays an important part in the initiation ceremonies of the mysteries. So too in the church of Jesus Christ.

Pagan gods and wise men were responsible for exactly the same miracles later to be claimed by the Jesus writers. Many of the earlier superheroes raised people from the dead, cured blindness, even turned water into wine; Pythagoras was the source of the fishing miracle, where he tells his disciples to cast a net in a different place and catch a net full of fish. Jesus does the same thing in the Gospel of John 21:4.

Dionysus, a righteous, just man, is hauled before the prosecutors and falsely accused, so too is Jesus.

The worshippers of the mysteries associated bread and wine with the body and the blood of the saviour, so too does the orthodox Church.

The ancient gods die a sacrificial death for their followers, so too does Jesus.

Crucifixion and hanging in a tree are mentioned in some of

the mystery cults, as it is in the Jesus story.

The sacrificed god spends a period in the underworld, as does Jesus.

The god resurrects or comes back to life after three days and usually at the time of our Easter, as does Jesus.

All of this and much more is quoted by historians in just about every book you can pick up that discusses the contents of the New Testament and the historicity, or not, of Jesus. It is certainly hard to refute but apologists still ignore some of the obvious conclusions and maintain that Christianity was a brand-new revelation, with a unique Saviour who came to save mankind; unlike all those pagans whose miracles were never as good as those of Jesus.

Chapter 6

Out of Egypt

When considering the pagan origins of the Old and New Testaments, a profound knowledge of the gods of Egypt and their life stories is essential.

It has been said that nothing that exists in the Bible that does not have some early foundation in the stories of ancient Egypt.

There is undoubtedly a lifetime of study to be found in the hundreds of heavy tomes dedicated to the myths of the people of Egypt from as far back as 4000 BCE.

The stories of their gods, their saviours, and of course, their Pharaohs, are truly complicated affairs and in this section of our quest, we can do little more than glean only a tiny part of that mythology, which may add some more substance to the origins of the Jesus story that is ever more elusive.

To read the Old Testament with its symbolic stories of ancient heroes, like Abraham, Moses, Joshua, Solomon and all those other names associated with the incredible tales of plagues, parting of waters and living a life of many hundreds of years, one would assume that this was written history.

There is not a single piece of archaeological evidence to confirm the existence of the Temple of Solomon or indeed, Solomon himself. The respected historian Philip Gardiner suggests in his work, *Gnosis: The Secrets of Solomon's Temple Revealed,* New Page Books, 2006:

"The Temple was merely a metaphor and never existed in reality."

This is startling stuff and quite explosive when you consider how much of Jewish history and their religious writings and ultimately, the Old Testament, is based on the lives of early characters, like Solomon.

The lack of conclusive evidence does not only apply to Solomon and his Temple, because the same can be said for all the other great characters too.

We have no convincing evidence for a man called Moses, other than the mythology we read in the Old Testament. There is no archaeological evidence for walls falling down at Jericho but it lives on in folklore.

What we do have are myths from previous cultures and civilisations, written on clay tablets and telling the same stories, later to be adapted by the Hebrews, for an account of their ancient "history".

The Great Flood in Genesis is predated by many centuries and so, too, is the story of Moses as a child floating in a basket to be found and cared for by a princess.

It sounds as though the Old Testament writers were, like their New Testament counterparts, not averse to a bit of borrowing and engaging in what in modern times would be regarded as downright plagiarism from previous civilizations, although such a concept did not exist in ancient religions.

We know so very little accurate history about the origins of the Old Testament: where and when the stories were written and the historical detail behind the main players in the epics. Everything seems to be based on legend and a desire to maintain a firm belief in a good tale that can be looked at as real history.

Do you really believe the story of Adam and Eve or is it a myth bathed in allegory? Do you believe there was a man called Noah who built a boat of specific dimensions to house the animals of the world during a particularly heavy rainstorm? Did people really live to the fantastic ages recorded in the Old Testament? Did a man called Jonah spend days inside a whale and then come out as though it was the natural thing to do?

Is the same to be said about Moses and the others? Or is the story of Moses and all the other gripping tales of daring, success and failure just another allegorical myth meant to symbolize a link between astrology, cosmic and agricultural cycles?

The stories of the Israelites coming out of Egypt and recorded in the Book of Exodus, tells the story of the liberation of the people from slavery in the 13th century BCE, led by their famous leader, Moses.

Exodus lays down the ingredients for the developing history of the nation and tells of the miraculous parting of the waters of the Red Sea or as some scholars state, is sometimes referred to as the Sea of Reeds and is mislocated as the Red Sea.

As a way of establishing the history of a people, it certainly does a good job. Lots of adventure, hardship, and miraculous stuff everywhere!

However, there is no archaeological evidence that any of this ever happened. Nothing to say conclusively that a man called Moses actually carried out these wondrous deeds, simply references to people and deeds in a book of symbolism, allegory and pure magic: the Old Testament.

The controversial scholar, author and historian, Ahmed Osman, has looked at the shadowy and early history of the Moses figure and come up with some startling and earth-shattering conclusions about the history of not only Moses but some of the other well-known names of the Old Testament.

It would be impossible to explain the work of Osman in the pages of our investigation but suffice to say, he makes a very plausible case for the fact that Moses never did exist, not as "Moses", but was in fact the Egyptian Akhenaten, who was banished from Egypt because of his worship of the one god, the Aten.

Most respected biblical Egyptologists reject Osman's hypotheses, however, they are equally unable to present any archaeological or documentative evidence to show the actual existence of Moses or any of the characters from early Jewish history.

Was Moses an invented figure?

We have much more historical evidence for the existence of the Egyptian pharaohs than any of the leaders and prophets of the Old Testament. The Egyptian tombs, hieroglyphs, and artefacts confirm the reality of these ancient god figures and on reading the Osman theories, it is easy to see how he was able to propose that the history of the early Jewish nation was, in fact, based on the histories of the Pharaohs of Egypt!

That influence carried through to the pages of the New Testament and as we have discussed earlier, there are some remarkable similarities to the myth of Osiris and Isis, when compared to the supposedly true story of Yeshua, or Jesus.

The worship of Osiris and of Isis played a massive part in the development of religious philosophy throughout the ancient world and it's probably worth taking a little time to understand the basic concept of the myth if we are to understand more about the effect it had on the gospel writers' views of the life of Jesus.

The elements of the story change through time and place but essentially it tells the myth of Osiris who was the great grandson of the Sun god Ra. He was the first Pharaoh and his queen Isis, was the first queen.

They ruled during a golden age and all was well in the world. That is, until the jealous brother Set, had desires not just on the throne, but on Isis and the power to rule the world as well.

He came up with a cunning plan. He planned to kill Osiris by building a magic box, a box that would trap anyone who entered it from escaping.

At the great Feast of the Gods, he tricked his brother into climbing into his box, and having done that, he locked it shut, sealed it with molten lead and hurled it into the River Nile, where it floated away with the body of Osiris inside it.

A jubilant Set claimed the throne and his queen, immediately the fortunes of the people took a turn for the worse. Wars and lawlessness reigned.

Osiris' faithful queen, Isis, launched a search for the body of her partner and having found it, brought it back to Egypt, where she placed it in the house of the gods.

She changes herself into a bird and flies around him, eventually perching on him where the spirit of the dead Osiris entered her and she gave birth to the baby Horus.

Isis, with the help of the wise man Thoth devised magic to bring him back to life but before they could cast their magic, the very nasty Set found the body and tore it into many pieces, scattering them all over the land of Egypt. With the help of her sister Nephthys, Isis was able to find all the parts of the body. (Some variations occur in the story at this point.) Having found the parts of the shredded body, Thoth and Anubis, the Lord of the Dead, were able to do a bit of hocus pocus magic and having cast the Ritual of Life magic, Osiris' spirit re-entered him and he resurrected.

Osiris lives on in the land of the dead, a place called Duat, where he stands in judgement on the souls of the deceased.

Horus grows from the holy child to be the avenger of his father, Osiris. Isis gives him magic powers and Thoth gives him the magic knife to use in his eternal battle against Set.

The battle between Set and Horus continues until Set, finally defeated by Horus, is cast into darkness, where he lives to this day. The battle is ongoing between Set as the Lord of Darkness and Horus the Lord of Light, the eternal battle of good and evil, light and dark.

Horus gives guidance to the Pharaoh in life, while Osiris watches over us in the hereafter.

Set is constantly seeking revenge and when he wins a battle, we are beset with turmoil and misery but when Horus wins the day, all is well in the world.

The myth goes on to tell that in the final days, the spirit of goodness, the Lord of Light, will win the battle and Set will be vanquished forever. Then, Osiris will return to earth, at the Day of awakening, when Osiris will allow the tombs of the righteous dead to break open and allow the bodies to come back to life.

A somewhat familiar story to the myth of the dead bodies springing out of the ground at the time of the crucifixion of Jesus!

A great story that would probably make a good mythical film.

In the myth described, there is only one form of a story that has many, many variations but at the root of them all is the same story of a just and righteous god figure who is badly treated, dies a cruel death as a result of evil doings and finally comes back with a promise that in the final days, he will return again to his faithful and happiness will once again, reign supreme. The biblical similarities become ever more obvious when the celebrations of the god are compared but it is the story of the avenging son Horus that brings this point home even more starkly.

Horus, depicted as a falcon headed man, or sometimes as a sphinx, appears in the Egyptian myth in a variety of different personas.

He appears as Harmakhet, known to the ancients as the God of the dawn and the morning Sun. In this variant, he is depicted as the sphinx and sometimes as the sphinx with the head of a ram.

In his manifestation as Har Pa Khered, he is shown as the nursing infant, on the lap of his mother, Isis, incredibly similar to the image of the Madonna and child and actually, very often confused with it.

As Horus of Edfu, he is God of the noonday Sun and battles endlessly with Set and his dark army, to ensure the Sun rises every day and as Ra-Harakhte, he becomes the great Sun god himself; the early pyramid texts refer to him in solar terms as God of the East.

We know from pyramid texts of the late Old Kingdom that the living king was identified as the earthly Horus and the dead king, as Osiris, his father. For reasons that will become obvious later, it should be noted that, as the Egyptologist, Dr J. Dunn at Cambridge University points out in an essay about the mythology behind the story of Horus, "Furthermore, Horus was combined, synchronized, and closely associated with deities such as the Sun god, Re."

He goes on to add, "The Eye of Horus must also be mentioned. The injury inflicted by Set on the eye of Horus is alluded to in the Pyramid Texts, where royal saliva is prescribed for its cure. The restored eye of Horus became the symbol for the state of soundness or perfection, known as the Udjat Eye. Used as an amulet, it became the symbol for protection and painted on the sides of rectangular coffins."

Do you remember the story of Jesus and even the Emperor, healing the eyes of the blind man by using his spittle? Where did that come from?

It's when we compare the lives of Horus and Jesus, from birth, that the resemblances become too much to be coincidence.

It is only fair to Christian apologists, to point out here, that some scholars doubt the existence of these incredible similarities, but they, too, have been criticised for not taking into account the many manifestations of the Horus figure.

Maybe even Matthew when writing his gospel was aware that what was said in Hosea 11:1, was pretty good as a useable prophecy, "Out of Egypt I called My Son" (Matthew 2:15).

Matthew probably realized the debt they owed to the Egyptian myths!

Great scholars like Gerald Massey (1828–1907), at the beginning of the twentieth century, were convinced that the mysteries of early Christianity had come as a direct result of the syncretism of the myths of Egypt with those of the Greeks, Persians and early Jewish sects. It was, for him, that the story of Jesus Christ as a saviour, was directly taken from the histories of the god Horus.

Massey's work *Ancient Egypt*, Martino Fine Books, 2014, has been widely rejected by some sections of the biblical academic world, whilst others have found his findings as invaluable, in the search for the Christian origins. Those that do not like the message often want to shoot the messenger.

Much of what Massey discusses is now accepted by many historians as elements of the story which must be taken seriously. Other scholars have taken up his work and expanded upon it and all point in a direction that places Egypt firmly in the frame when looking for clues to the historical Jesus.

The work of the historian D.M. Murdock (1960–2015), also known under her pen name as Acharya S. is essential reading for those people who want to pursue the Egyptian links. Her book *Christ in Egypt: The Horus Jesus Connection*, Stellar House Publishing, 2009, is a masterpiece of research, using highly respected primary sources to demonstrate that the Christian message has its roots in many cultures around the globe and, very much so, in the land of Egypt.

My own research on the similarities of the deities, certainly surprised me, as the story unfolded of an Egyptian god figure that could easily be Jesus in another guise.

Let us have a look at some of the rather uncomfortable comparisons that apologists find hard to refute but resolutely continue to do so.

As long ago as when Massey was publishing his findings, he was telling people even then that Horus was born of a supernatural birth, He was the Son of God. His mother was the goddess Isis, also known as Meri, (Mary?), He was of royal descent and he was born in a cave at the Winter Solstice (late December). His birth was marked by a star and in some accounts, attended by shepherds.

It goes on, He was part of the Holy trinity, Seb was His earth father, (compare with Joseph as earth father of Jesus) and Seb was a carpenter! He was baptized by Anup the Baptizer, He was regarded as the Good shepherd and depicted with a shepherd's crook. There is a story of Horus feeding the multitude at Annu. In some accounts there is evidence of Horus having disciples, though not twelve. (The twelve disciples followed the pattern of the twelve tribes of Israel in Jewish mythology?)

Massey also mentions that Horus ascends to the Egyptian heaven from the Mount of the olive tree!

The similarities can be listed, literally, in the hundreds, when all the ingredients of the story, like titles and astrological associations and the "I Am " statements are looked at.

Horus was known as the Krst or anointed one as Jesus was the Christ, or anointed one, and his depiction as Horus the infant in the arms of his holy mother Meri (Isis), is identical to that of Jesus and Mary.

The similarities really do go on and on! In his manifestation as a Sun god, Amen-Ra, is it possible that his name influenced the Christian word "Amen" after prayers?

This is most certainly a myth that the founders of early Christianity were acquainted with.

The Egyptian influence from the very earliest of times, from the time of Moses, through all those patriarchal figures and ultimately into the pages of the New Testament, is glaringly obvious to all but those who wish to ignore the unpalatable truth.

It is simply not possible for an ancient civilisation like that of ancient Israel, living next to and in such close association to Egypt, not to have absorbed so much of its history.

The history of Egypt is rich and is there for all to see. Their gods and Pharaohs are depicted in amazing detail on the walls of their tombs in the pyramids, which we can visit to this day. We know their religious beliefs and their mythical gods too, from archaeology. The pottery tells stories of the Sun gods, the falcon headed god, Horus, the mysteries of Isis and the life stories of some of the most famous of the rulers of the early dynasties. In fact, we know, reliably, that they existed.

We have none of this reliable evidence for a history of life and death, or even an existence, of the biblical supermen, like Moses or Joseph or Joshua. No tombs, no archaeology, nothing to compare to what we can use in the Egyptian example.

Is it possible that what we discussed earlier, the theory that is postulated by Ahmed Osman, that the history of early Israel is actually a complicated mix involving the real characters of ancient Egypt? He suggests Akhenaten is the basis for the mythical character and the eventual historical character Moses of the Old Testament. On the face of it, it sounds a convincing argument but regardless of how you see it, it can no longer be denied that the Egyptian culture most certainly found its way into the creative mythology of a lot of the early Hellenized Judaism that ultimately became the New Testament story of today.

If the Horus influence and that of his Egyptian relatives has shocked and surprised you, just wait until we look a little further afield and take on board the similarities that exist between Jesus and the life stories of the far older deities, Buddha, and Krishna.

Chapter 7

Buddha and Krishna Leave Their Mark

I am fully convinced that the Egyptian myth made an indelible mark on the pages of later Jewish and Christian writings; but there were other influences.

We started our journey by considering the melting pot of cultures that was the Mediterranean at the end of the first century CE. At this time and into the second century, the gospel compilers were busily penning their ideas about the life of the Saviour.

At this time, too, the cultures of the Greeks, the Jews, the Persians, and the Egyptians had already made their mark on the religious myths and gods, commonly worshipped by the faithful and they were aware of another philosophy that had permeated their society, certainly in Alexandria, that which had arrived from the East.

The trade routes of the time had made the cultures of India and beyond something that would be well known in the centres of trade and learning, just like Alexandria.

As a centre of spiritual learning and the cults of the Gnostics, one, two or even all four of the gospels may well have been written here, and the stories from all over the Empire and far beyond certainly did find their way into the account of the Saviour's life and works.

To deny this in the face of such evidence is dismissive. Why do Christians who are literalists, those that believe the stories in the Bible in a true, in a literal sense, consider the accretions of other cultures onto their revelation, such a bad thing anyway? Maybe at the time of the writing of the gospels, it was what they all did? Maybe everybody knew the business of syncretism and it wasn't such a big issue to them as it is to us today?

It was in this climate that the stories of Buddha had arrived on the streets of Alexandria.

We know from early historians of the presence of a Jewish sect called the Therapeutae, who were referred to by the famous historian Philo (25 BCE–50 CE).

Philo describes how they lived and from the description, they could easily have been Buddhist monks. Even their name comes from a Buddhist origin.

In Robert Linssen's work *Zen Living*, Grove Press,1994, reference is made to the Buddhist proselytising at the time of King Ashoka (260–218 BCE) according to the Edicts of Asoka, and this points very definitely to a Buddhist presence in the Mediterranean and in Alexandria.

We will be looking much closer at the Therapeutae a little later, as they seem to have played a major role in the developing story of Christianity.

The historian J.H. Bentley, when referring to the Buddhist influence on the gospels says,

"They (scholars) have often considered the possibility that Buddhism influenced the early development of Christianity. They have drawn attention to many parallels concerning the births, lives, doctrines, and deaths of the Buddha and Jesus" (*Cross Cultural Contacts and Exchanges in Pre-Modern Times*, Oxford University Press ,1992).

Well, with a comment like that, you can see what is about to follow! The Jesus story was evident in the myth of Horus and it is also very obvious in the myth of Buddha.

So much of what was said and performed by Jesus, was demonstrated by the Buddha, five hundred years earlier.

The list of life similarities is remarkable and for the reader who wants to pursue this line of study further, they should read the work of Marcus Borg *Jesus and Buddha: The Parallel Sayings*, Ulysses Press, 1997,Acharya S's *Suns of God: Krishna, Buddha and Christ Unveiled*, Adventures Unlimited Press, 2004, or any other works by D.M. Murdock.

Some writers have tried to imply that during the "lost" years of Jesus' life, that is before his arrival on the scene at age thirty, he may well have travelled in the distant lands of India and learnt the teachings and philosophy of Buddha and used them in his own teachings. If so, why does the Bible story not relate to it and why does Paul not mention it?

Let us have a look at some of those things that cause problems for the apologists for the similarities of the life of Jesus with that of Buddha.

The various myths of the Buddha tell us:

- he was born of a miraculous birth and in some accounts, a virgin birth,
- his birth was attended by angelic figures,
- wise men were aware of the birth,
- he spent 40 days in the wilderness,
- he was tempted by the Devil figure,
- he began his ministry at the age of thirty,
- he had a group of disciples,
- one of his followers betrayed him,
- he was "baptized" in the holy river,
- he travelled and performed miracles,
- he cured blindness,
- he gave up worldly goods for a simple life,
- he preached the philosophy of love and peace,
- he entered in triumph into the city of Rajagriha,
- he walked on water,
- he conducted teachings on a mount, and
- his death was accompanied by supernatural happenings.

This is just a sample of the very many comparisons quoted by scholars and it's not only those life comparisons we should be aware of but, amazingly, even the sayings and moral outlooks were almost mirror images of each other.

Jesus taught that "a foolish man builds his house on the sand." Five hundred years before Buddha was preaching, "Perishable is the city built of sand."

The sayings of Jesus mirrored by Buddha are just too numerous to be coincidental. Sayings such as,

"Do to others as you would have them do to you" (Jesus in Luke 6:31).

"Consider others as yourself"(Buddha Dhammapada 10:1).

"If anyone strikes you on the cheek, offer the other also" (Jesus in Luke 6:29).

"If anyone should give you a blow with his hand, with a stick or with a knife, you should abandon any desires and utter no evil words" (Buddha, Majjhima Nikaya 21:6).

"Everyone who lives and believes in me will never die" (Jesus in John 11:26).

"Those who have sufficient faith in me, sufficient love for me, are all headed for heaven or beyond" (Buddha, Majjhima Nikaya 22:47).

"And after six days Jesus takes with him, Peter and James and John and leads them up into a high mountain apart by themselves. And he was transfigured before them. And his raiment became shining, exceeding white as snow, so no fuller on earth can white them" (Mark 9:2).

"Ananda, having arranged one set of golden robes on the body of the Lord (Buddha), observed that against the Lord's body it appeared dulled. And he said, 'it is wonderful Lord, it is marvellous how clear and bright the Lord's skin appears! It looks even brighter than the golden robes in which it is clothed'" (Buddha, Digha Nikaya 16:4:37).

I have found more than twenty sayings of Buddha, which are used centuries later by Jesus. There are undoubtedly many more.

The Buddhist influence permeates the gospels throughout

and certainly has a major influence in the Gnostic gospels of the very early Christians.

The brilliant Danish scholar of Buddhism and Sanskrit Dr Christian Lindtner (1949–2020) has his own firm ideas about Buddhism and Christianity, and states unequivocally "that the gospels, perhaps even the New testament as a whole, is a pirate copy of the Buddhist gospels, or of the Buddha's testament" (www.jesusbuddha.com).

When somebody of such academic standing says something like this, we really should be listening.

He makes another highly significant point, too, about something we mentioned in an earlier chapter. You may remember that we spoke about a source used by the gospel writers, which was never discovered and was known as the Q (Quelle) Source.

Christian Lindtner's theory is that that source was taken directly from the Buddhist texts of the Mulasarvastivada Vinaya and the Saddharmapundarika.

He also has conclusive evidence from the original Sanskit texts that the Q source, which was supposedly directly responsible for the gospel accounts, was originally a composite of two of the main Buddhist texts.

Lindtner is one of the most highly respected Sanskrit scholars in his field and his theory, if proved correct, will undoubtedly devastate the foundations of the Church; that is if modern orthodox Church leaders were to be open to proper academic scrutiny of the origins of the New Testament.

For a truly academic and profound analysis of the Buddhist texts and the gospel parallels, the work of Albert J. Edmunds M.A. (1857–1941) in *Buddhist and Christian gospels*, The Library of the University of Toronto, 1914, (Classic Reprint Series – forgottenbooks.com) is essential reading. It is edited with English notes on Chinese versions, dating from the early Christian centuries by the renowned scholar Masaharu Anesaki (1873–

1949), Professor of Religious Science at Imperial University of Tokyo and Professor of Japanese Literature at Harvard.

I stress the academic qualifications of the scholars behind this work because it is still a problem for many orthodox members of the Church to accept what is being claimed about the Buddha/Jesus similarities.

In the work of Herbert Cutner (1881–1969): *Jesus: God, Man or Myth?*, Society of Metaphysicians, 1999, he notes how Christianity has spread around the globe but has never really "conquered".

We still see huge swathes of the earth where Islam, Buddhism and Hinduism are the principal religious faiths.

I was discussing this with a Hindu community leader, and I asked what impression Christianity had made in India. He answered light heartedly that it was not very significant because they already had their own version of the faith in the story of their Hindu Krishna.

He said so much of the Jesus story was reflected in tales of the Krishna that there was nothing very new.

We have looked at the lives of so many of the forerunners of Jesus, including Horus and Buddha, all worshipped centuries before the Christian godman.

The Hindu God Krishna, like Jesus, is the second person of a holy trinity. He is an incarnation of the god Vishnu and he is believed by his followers to have lived in the third century BCE. Some myths claim his birth occurred as far back as 3228 BCE.

So much in the life of Krishna is familiar and was noted by the American mid-nineteenth-century freethinker and writer Kersey Graves (1813–1883), who listed more than three hundred common elements between the two. He was, however, a little too enthusiastic and several of those comparisons were later shown not to be accurate. Work by later writers and certainly by those of the present day and, I would mention again, the books of D.M. Murdock (Acharya S), are conclusive in their findings.

Kersey Graves listed the following credible comparisons between Krishna and Christ, that:

- both were Sons of God,
- both had adoptive fathers who were carpenters,
- both were of royal descent,
- wise men, shepherds, and a star figure occur in both births,
- a local bad man planned to kill both holy children,
- both spent time in the wilderness,
- both were considered human and divine,
- both are associated with a resurrection,
- both performed miracles and healed lepers,
- both raised the dead,
- both claim a miraculous birth,
- both taught forgiveness, and
- both spent time in their mythical hell.

The findings of other later scholars point to so much more that cannot be ignored: for example, Krishna's birth happens when his foster father is travelling to another city to pay his taxes.

The respected French writer and collector of Sanskrit myths Louis Jacolliot (1837–1890) relates to the story of Krishna being hanged in a tree by his murderer in *The Bible in India*, Sun Pub Co., 1992.

Do you remember that confusing business of Jesus hanging in a tree or was it a cross or does the term "hanging on" and "in a tree" mean the same thing?

And so, the comparisons goes on.

In our search for an historical Jesus, a figure that was both a Christ and a man, and indeed, the living God on earth, we have already looked at a variety of important, usually unknown elements, to the development of the story.

In mentioning in some depth, the history of the Mysteries,

the lives of Horus, Buddha, and Krishna, I hope you, like me, when I discovered these truths, may by now be looking at the Jesus adventures with a somewhat different attitude.

I am trying to keep my investigation on a readable but not too simplistic level. There are huge numbers of books available out there, written by scholars in their field who can and do discuss the theology behind most of the pre-Christian mythology and the early Church history, in a depth that defies the understanding of the average reader. So much so, in fact, that I sometimes wonder if they can't see the proverbial wood for the trees!

The defenders of the faith will use any theological get-out to deny the blatantly obvious conclusions that have been drawn by academics who assess the facts as presented and plainly see the situation, that the New Testament is not a historical account of a God who came to earth and lived and walked amongst us.

Christian apologists will sneer at those who demonstrate the absurdity of the biblical claims. If you are a regular Bible reader, just think again for a moment about the ridiculous, supernatural events that occur regularly throughout the pages.

People live to be hundreds of years old, prophets fly off into the sky on chariots, voices come out of the sky, five thousand people are fed with a couple of fishes, zombies leap out of the ground and come back to life. Do you believe it? Do you believe that water really turned into wine at a wedding, that very dead people were brought back to life and that a devil figure was able to converse with a living God and the words spoken were recorded for us? But by whom? Did a young virgin become pregnant by the magic of a Jewish tribal God, the same "kindly" God that thought nothing of slaying anybody that does not see things his way?

Scholars of a mind to confirm the veracity of this stuff, know that it is easy to keep the public on their side because the story they tell is exactly what we were all taught at school and so, they believe, we would support their opinions wouldn't we?

They know that the general populous does not know the facts. The orthodox scholars, are fully aware of the factual information stacking up against their arguments; many even say that some of the biblical history is actually allegory and not necessarily truly historical. How do they choose which is myth and which is "true"?

Quite simply, they pick and choose as they see fit. Nothing of what is written has any historical evidence to support it, that is, no historical evidence that is accepted by the academic world as genuine and incredible, often amongst their own academic ranks as well.

I remember reading a piece of advice offered by a supposedly scholarly supporter of the Christian story who told his readers that when they were confronted with the sort of unanswerable detail we have discussed, they should smile at their detractor, open their eyes wide and say, " You don't really believe that do you?"

This is not what I would call a profound argument!

Chapter 8

Voicing the Doubts

At this point, I think we should return to our friend the apostle Paul who is reputedly responsible for the instigation of this whole saga.

You may remember we left Paul after he had a dream or vision of a saviour figure that he perceived as the long-awaited Messiah.

None of the Jesus story was known to Paul at his time because what you have read in these pages about births and miracles, baptising, bodily resurrection, and every other aspect that became the gospel story of a godman amongst us, had yet to be created.

Critics will say that it was common knowledge, a word-of-mouth story that had astounded the masses and there was no need to write it down. It simply does not stand up historically and we will look at that history a little later.

Paul had a vision of a supernatural being, a spirit, a god figure who was in heaven. God had chosen Paul as the messenger to spread the word that the Saviour was, at last, about to appear.

It was this spirit in Paul's head that ultimately became the Jesus Christ figure of today's followers.

Reading about Paul in the Epistles and then comparing him to Paul in Acts, you may begin to think that we are reading about two very different people and it has been suggested that that is exactly the case. The Bible is full of contradictions, dozens and dozens of contradictions, and so it is with the stories related about Paul and his mission.

It is probably worth taking more note of what he says himself as possibly a bit more reliable and always bearing in mind that what we read today, as the New Testament, has been tampered with repeatedly during the centuries since it was compiled. We simply do not know what the story was in the original works, and that includes the Letters of Paul. Christian scribes have without doubt added their own opinions to so much of what they were reproducing that we really do not know what the very earliest story about the life of Jesus really told us.

As we said in an earlier chapter, scholars appear to agree that the Epistles of Paul do seem to be the earliest of the New Testament texts and yet, even they have been altered and added to.

Only seven of the writings of Paul have been considered genuine and of those, there are doubts about three of them.

When Paul speaks about the Christ figure that he met with in his vision, he is talking like a Gnostic.

You will remember from our first chapter that there was a sect of philosophical thinkers who applied their reasoning to religious concepts. These were what we call today the Gnostic Christians.

I would remind you again that unless we have a knowledge of this early philosophy, we will never understand the thinking behind the origins of the Jesus story.

I said, too, that the Gnostic Christians pursued their religious belief in parallel with the orthodox Christians, but the Gnostic concept did not develop from the orthodox faith, it actually existed in another form, centuries before the Gnostics of the first century accepted the figure of Yeshua or Jesus as their Christ and teacher.

Gnosticism came out of Zoroastrianism, Judaism, Platonism and without doubt, from the religious philosophy of Egypt. To that you can add the Hellenistic concepts of the mystery religions, the net result being what we described as demonstrated by the many sects which we discussed earlier.

Paul in his words and writings casts himself firmly in the Gnostic camp.

Read the Epistles of Paul and you will agree that it is hard to argue with the fact that he sees the Jesus figure as a Christ, that is, a spiritual divine being but only in spirit.

Throughout our journey so far, I have been a little too casual with the names and titles that have been ascribed to Jesus Christ. As a man, he is Jesus but as the resurrected Divine Saviour, he is Christ the Messiah, he is God.

It is important to use the correct title depending on which aspect of the Divine being we are relating to.

In Paul's case, he refers exclusively to the Christ figure. The Divine figure he perceives is the spirit of the resurrected Christ, in heaven, alongside God. Paul does not relate to a Jesus figure born in Bethlehem of the Virgin Mary and has no interest or, indeed, any knowledge of the magnificent deeds carried out by the man figure of Jesus. Paul's Christ was a spirit and if you read the letters of Paul closely, you will have to agree that his Jesus Christ had no earthliness.

This is how so many of the Gnostic thinkers saw their divine teacher in the religious schools of pre-Christian and early Christian times.

To refer again to our original discussion regarding the Gnostics – they searched for the divine within ourselves and this is what the Gnostic Christians did also.

Many of them did not believe in a walking, talking Jesus, as described in the gospels in the New Testament. For them it was a Divine Spirit who was their teacher and for Paul, Jesus was the Christ who was able to fulfil this role and more. Jesus Christ was the Messiah who would return to earth very soon and save mankind.

The Christ of Paul's vision was a figment of his imagination based, maybe, on something that he expected and probably hoped would eventually come along and fulfil his desires to announce the imminent arrival of the Messiah.

Much scholarly debate has been going on for a century and more about the nature and identity of the figure brought to life in the imagination of Paul.

The gospels were still to be written and this is probably why Paul has no interest or awareness of the life story so well known to us today. Consider this, Paul preaches the story of a Saviour who as the Son of God, will soon be amongst the brethren and the faithful will be saved and rewarded with everlasting life.

He talks about the crucifixion of his godman. He talks about the resurrection, but he does not tell us the most basic details of when, or where.

He gives no indication that this Saviour was a man who walked around Palestine bringing people back to life, healing sick people, doing amazing deeds that were equal to the miracles of the gods of the Mystery Religions.

Bible scholars find it hard to answer these problems and I have never yet read a convincing reason for why Paul has ignored every single element of the life of the living Jesus.

With no information about the most basic aspects of his life, and no indication about when the crucifixion took place or where it took place, apart from a few phrases that have been shown to be forgeries and interpolations, we can only assume that Paul is relating to a redeeming saviour figure that lived in the distant past.

Paul himself admits to having been in the presence of the Apostles, Peter and James and yet still does not pick up on any piece of useful history that would give credibility and, especially time and place, to his Jesus character.

Paul's accounts of everything related to the very earliest story of the "appearance" of Jesus Christ have absolutely no convincing historical evidence, whatsoever, to give us even a hint of the historical nature of the most important man that ever "walked" the earth.

We have, at an earlier chapter, covered the point about the five hundred witnessing the risen Christ: exactly like the risen Buddha was witnessed by five hundred of his monks. Surely that gives the story some credibility. If that story were true and had happened at the time of the supposed resurrection, the great historians of the day would have written pages about it. Both Philo and Josephus could not have ignored the story of a Son of God, dead for three days and then seen by more than five hundred followers. They did ignore it because it never happened like that. Was it Paul who wrote these words? Was it a later interpolation or Paul's way of saying that the faithful and the main apostles had dreams and visions of the hero figure that they revered from a distant past?

Some scholars have long suspected that there was, in the years before the arrival of Christianity, a Jewish cult that worshipped a divine being named Yeshua and it was this Jesus or Yeshua that Paul related to in his visions.

It is an interesting point to note that the name Yeshua or Jesus as we translate it means "saviour". You can understand why the later gospel writers could not have their Saviour called anything else other than Jesus.

Several suggestions have been made by worthy scholars as to who this pre-existent Yeshua was and it is at this point that we should delve a little deeper into those characters, the scholars who discuss them and the Jewish cult or cults who were active at the time of the early first century and were probably responsible for the eventual rise of Christianity.

By now, you are probably aware that I have, after many years of analysing the evidence, come to my own conclusion that the Jesus Christ of the New Testament is a mythical figure and was never meant to be considered as a human godman, passing amongst us doing miraculous things. Paul only saw his Christ as a spiritual being and the human man was a much later development.

The mythicist position has been heavily criticized by biblical scholars, who almost universally, are Christian scholars anyway. They do, to give many of them credit, admit that there are serious issues about the lack of information regarding the historical detail about Jesus but nevertheless, cannot admit that the Jesus character is purely mythical.

As far back as the eighteenth century serious doubts about the existence of an historical Jesus were being raised by two well-known French philosophers Charles Francois Dupuis (1742–1809) and Constantin-Francois Chasseboeuf, Comte de Volney, (1757–1820).

Dupuis totally rejected the reference by the Roman historian Tacitus in the second century CE, to a man called Christus, which he claimed was nothing but an echo of the inaccurate beliefs of the Christians at that time.

He considered the Jesus figure of the gospels to be a creation of astrological elements and solar worship.

Volney suggested in his work *Les Ruines* that the Jesus figure was an obscure historical character whose life was integrated with solar mythology. Napoleon, a friend of Volnay, is quoted as saying that the existence of Jesus was an open question.

The well-known Scottish writer and advocate of the Jesus myth J.M Robertson (1856–1933), believed there was a pre-existent divine figure who was similarly revered by sects such as the Ebionites and the Nazarenes, this figure was Joshua or Yeshua of the Old Testament. These groups had worshipped the memory of the biblical Joshua and saw him as a future Messiah.

Robertson argued that the Epistles of Paul tell us absolutely nothing about Jesus and the subsequent gospels that turned him into a teacher and wonder worker were later developments amongst the Gentiles, who equally, would have taken many of the pagan myths as a core for their life story.

You may remember what we said earlier about the elements common to so many of the religious cults. The healing stories of Jesus may have come directly from the myths of Asclepius and Apollonius of Tyana, the feeding of the five thousand from the story of Dionysus, and the ability of being able to walk on water from the myths of Poseidon and, maybe, the Buddha.

The American Professor of Mathematics and proponent of the Jesus myth William Benjamin Smith (1850–1934), also postulated the idea of a pre-Christian Jesus or Yehsua cult involving the Nazarene sect that existed long before the time of the New Testament Jesus. The historical life of this figure was invented later by the gospel writers using the Old Testament expectations of the divine.

The much-respected scholar of his day Arthur Drews (1865–1935), Professor of Philosophy at Technische Hochschule in Karlsruhe, Germany, put forward the highly controversial view for his time that the Jesus myth grew out of Jewish Gnosticism and the Christ came out of Greek philosophy and the numerous myths of the dying and resurrecting deities of the mysteries.

The French Scholar and Medic Paul Louis Couchoud (1879–1959), in his works *The Enigma of Jesus, The Mystery of Jesus,* and *Jesus, the God Made Man* was firmly convinced that the Jesus of Paul's Epistles was a figment of his imagination and was the result of a new interpretation of ancient texts.

When Paul witnessed his Christ, not in the flesh as he admits himself but, only as a divine vision, he was at the time moving amongst the sects of the Ebionites and the Nazarenes and others, all of whom had expectations of a Messianic figure who had, at some time in the distant past, been a revered teacher in their early history.

The Joshua character of the Old Testament certainly figured with the Jewish sects of this time.

The question must be asked that if Paul arrived on the scene sharing his visions with those of the apostles of the sects with whom he was associated, and then went on to spread his evangelism amongst the Jews of the diaspora, why did they apparently not ask questions as to who this saviour godman was?

It would seem that they already knew who he was: the One

they had anticipated from a previous existence, the One whom they were already spiritually acquainted with – the Joshua or Jesus of their early history.

We keep mentioning the fact that the gospels had still not created an earthly life for this visionary being, therefore we must ask ourselves if the fine details of Mary, Joseph, miracles, bodily resurrection, angels, wise men, Mary Magdalene, zombies coming back to life and walking through the streets, would have been common knowledge anyway without the need for Paul to relate it to the listening faithful.

I think not. If this visionary Messiah was the Jesus of Matthew, Mark, Luke and John, then all that information would have to have been in circulation; but how?

Neither Paul, nor any other first-century texts outside the gospels relate to a living Jesus, with detail of his life and miracles. If no questions were asked and Paul certainly did not provide any information, then you can only conclude that they already knew it all.

The argument certainly does look as though the message was received by Jews who already had a traditional knowledge of their expected, revered prophet and it was Paul who announced the imminent arrival: their Messiah was not the Jesus Christ that played the role in the gospels, many years later. The Jesus of Paul and the Jesus of the gospels were two very different characters. The gospel Jesus was a mythical character created for political reasons and to give substance to a story that certainly lacked it, when you look at Paul's way of telling the tale and, indeed, everybody else's in the middle years of the first century.

It would be remiss not to mention the truly scholarly works of G.A. Wells (1926–2017), who was Professor of German at the University of London. In his books *Did Jesus Exist?* Prometheus,1975; *The Jesus Legend*, Open Court, 1996; *The Jesus Myth*, Open Court, 1999; and *Cutting Jesus Down to Size*, Open Court, 2009.

Wells argues convincingly that the earliest Christian texts from the first century CE do not relate to the gospel traditions of the preaching miracle worker of recent decades. Rather they present him, "As a basically supernatural personage, only obscurely on earth as a man at some unspecified period in the past" (G.A. Wells, "Earliest Christianity", infidels.org., 1999).

In the world of scholarly debate, Wells attracts much criticism and an equal amount of praise. The conservative theologians who are firmly in the literal truth camp, demonize him, while those of a more liberal nature see the value of his profound argument.

Professor Michael Martin (1932–2015), Corpus Christi College, Oxford, points out "Wells' argument against the historicity of Jesus is sound."

The American Reverend Dr Robert M. Price is another of the regular big names that offers convincing arguments regarding the historicity question. Price, an American New Testament scholar, is a former Baptist pastor who became disillusioned with the arguments put forward by Christian apologists; the series of books *Deconstructing Jesus*, Prometheus, 2000; *The Incredible Shrinking Son of Man*, Prometheus, 2003; and *Jesus Is Dead*, American Atheist Press, 2007, are essential reading for anybody wishing to approach the question on a deeper, scholarly level.

He believes the Christian origins came about because of the synthesis of Jewish, Greek and Egyptian mythology and suggests the myths of the Gods, Baal, Osiris, Adonis, Attis and Tammuz played a major part in influencing those origins.

He also points out that defenders of the Christian story have tried to minimize these parallels.

It is often quoted that the gospels were never meant to be read as historical documents and this only came into being at a much later date. Those who understood the deeper symbolism never read the texts literally. They were allegorical and concealed a deeper meaning within. It was almost as though some of the gospels on an outer level were stories for children, while on a deeper, more profound level, they revealed truths about Christ. The feeding of the multitudes is a good example, of which, more later.

Professor Thomas L. Thompson, retired Professor of Theology at University of Copenhagen, is another academic who denies the existence of Jesus. In his work *The Messiah Myth*, Vintage, 2005, he argues that the stories of Jesus developed as a result of the combination of Near Eastern myths, he makes the point that gospel readers at the time would have understood this and that the stories were never intended as history.

The research of Professor Alvar Ellegard (1919–2008), of the University of Gothenburg, made a big impression on me and my own concepts about the historical origins of the Christian beginnings. For further reading, I recommend his book *Jesus – One Hundred Years Before Christ: A Study in Creative Mythology*, Overlook Press, 1999.

He, like many others believed that Paul's vision was of a prophet figure from an earlier age and was the teacher and prophet from a Jewish sect called the Essenes. It was the Essenes and their mystical belief system that may have been the main reason that Christianity eventually developed.

Chapter 9

The Mystical Essenes

The Essenes are an integral part of my investigation and we should look more at who they were and how they lived if we are to begin to understand how the Jesus Christ myth ultimately developed.

We know of the existence of the Jewish sect of the Essenes through the writings of historians who were recording events at the time of the mid to late first century CE.

Philo of Alexandria was a Hellenistic Jewish philosopher who was alive at the time of the Jesus story. His philosophy was based on the fusion of Greek philosophy and Judaism, which may have had some considerable influence on early Christian thought.

Philo recorded events of his time and he mentions the sect of the Essenes in his work "Quod Omnis Probus Liber Sit" which means "every good man is free".

He describes a group of ascetic Jews who dedicated their whole lives to the service of God. He numbered them in Palestine and Syria at about four thousand, but of course we have no confirmation of these estimates.

He refers to them as pious men who shared everything in common and tended to live in communities away from the lawlessness of the cities. They were of a peaceful nature and he makes the point that they would never be found involved in the making of arrows, javelins, or swords.

They totally rejected animal sacrifice and slavery and taught the love of God, the love of virtue and the love of mankind.

They studied their biblical texts and discussed at length the meaning within and believed in the adherence of looking on the deity as the cause of everything which is good and of nothing which is evil.

He describes in some detail as to how they reject worldly goods and shared absolutely everything in their community, which included food, houses, tables and clothes.

There is a suggestion that they were totally celibate, but history shows that some of their communities did include women. Philo also tells us that they cared for their sick in the community and the elderly and everything they did was for the common good.

In effect, the monastic ideal was alive and well!

The group is also recorded by the Jewish historian Flavius Josephus (38–107 CE), who mentions their existence around 103 BCE.

Josephus, one of the great historians of the day, describes similar characteristics to what we read from Philo and tells us that they are Jews by race but adds, "these men live the same kind of life which among the Greeks has been ordered by Pythagoras".

Josephus, too, talks about their ascetic lifestyle and their communal meals and very interestingly, describes their veneration for the Sun.

The sharing of everything and the study of their ancient literature is repeated by Josephus and he goes on to tell us that it is only after a period of three years that a new member, if considered worthy enough, would be able to become a full member of the community.

An interesting point for us is "they believe that their souls are immortal but that their bodies are corruptible". They believed in a place where the souls of the just would gather and they also believed in a hell (Flavius Josephus, *The Jewish War; The Jewish Antiquities*).

Pliny the Elder, a Roman writer of the time, (23–79 CE), included more information about the sect in his work *Natural History* and Hippolytus of Rome, writing two hundred years later, describes much of what Josephus recorded, but added some other material. As he was not an eyewitness, his account is not as reliable as that of Philo and Josephus.

Philo's *De Vita Contemplativa* describes another monastic ascetic sect, which has been related to the Essene sect in some quarters.

This group, who settled above Lake Mareotis near Alexandria, were named by him as the Therapeutae. They displayed some similarities to the Essene way of life but differed in as much as women participated in the activities of the Therapeutae and seemed to live a more contemplative life than the Essenes, who he describes as being more practical and active.

Theologically, they interpreted the Old Testament only allegorically and vocationally, they professed the art of healing, not only bodies, but souls too. That they were in some way related to the Essenes is not agreed by all scholars, but there is a body of opinion that links the two groups. To complicate matters even more, there were two other groups with links to the Essenes. These were the Ebionites and the Nazoraeans who like the Therapeutae, appear to have shared a Gnostic philosophy.

These early sects are important to know because it is from them and probably the Essenes, that the Christian cult eventually developed.

In fact, so Christian-like were the Therapeutae, that the church father Eusebius (260–340 CE), was convinced that they were Christians before Christianity had even been created.

In modern times the sect of the Essenes has come into the public arena as a result of the discovery in 1947 of the now famous Dead Sea Scrolls, which were found in a series of caves around the ancient settlement of Qumran on the shores of the Dead Sea.

These ancient texts have had a huge influence on our understanding of the way of life of the Jewish people who wrote them, and hid them for us to find nearly two thousand years later.

Like the Gnostic gospels, which were found at Nag Hammadi in Egypt only two years before, they appear to have been written and hidden as a way of saving for posterity, the life and times of the people who created them, because of the uncertainty of the dangerous times they were living in.

We could and indeed should, expand our study at this point, to take in the huge amount of material and significance that the discovery of the Scrolls had for Christianity. Unfortunately, it is a book in itself and we can only look at the vital details.

For readers wishing to study deeper on this topic, I recommend you start with the works of the Oxford scholar Geza Vermes (1924–2013), whose knowledge of the subject is legendary.

The scrolls have almost universally been ascribed to the Essenes who were living their monastic life at Qumran between 200 BCE and 70 CE, when the Roman army destroyed the Jerusalem Temple. Whether the scrolls were written at Qumran or brought there for safe keeping at the time of the Jewish Roman war, is open to debate.

The manuscripts, some found only as fragments, amount to about eight hundred scrolls, the content of which is both biblical and non-biblical.

The scrolls are the oldest group of Old Testament texts ever found and include all books of the Hebrew Bible, except the Book of Esther. The Isaiah Scroll is nearly a thousand years older than any previously known copy.

Significantly, there is no mention at all of any of the Christian writings of the mid first century and no mention is made of Jesus Christ of the gospels, None!

The non-biblical scrolls give a sharp insight as to how the Essenes lived as a community and give us much information about their history at the time.

They describe themselves as the "Sons of Light", the "Poor", the "Holy Ones" and members of the "Way".

Their enemies were the "Sons of Darkness", and we see the group as being messianic, apocalyptic, and a Jewish sect showing a new covenant.

At the time of the find, the Scrolls caused a major upheaval in the world of biblical scholarship. It was many years before anything was released about the findings within the manuscripts, with accusations made that because they did not carry the Christian message that was hoped for and expected, they were suppressed. Heavy tomes have been written on this one aspect of the story.

As far as we are concerned, we should take note of two main elements that have come out of the find.

We must consider the fact that one of the discoveries of the Scrolls demonstrate the fact that the Essenes were much involved with the apocalyptic literature of the Book of Enoch, which written during the second century BCE, is an extremely important non canonical apocryphal work, because of the influence it had on the origins of Christianity.

It is full of Gnostic teaching, such as concepts, stories of angels and visions of Heaven and Hell. It is here that we read about the Fallen Angels, the Watchers, Messiahs, resurrection and an end of times with the arrival of the Heavenly Kingdom. Even more, there is reference to astronomy, cosmology, and calendar systems. The Essenes were aware of all of this.

We should mention here that all writers of the New Testament were equally aware of the Book of Enoch and were almost certainly influenced by it in thought and written word (*Apocalyptic Literature, Encyclopaedia Biblica: A Critical Dictionary of the Literary, Political and Religious History, the Archaeology, Geography and Natural History of the Bible, Thomas Kelly Cheyne, John Sutherland Black,* published by Adam and Charles Black, 1902).

It cannot be underestimated how much influence that

this work would have had on the religious thought of the Essenes and the doctrines relating to the Messiah, the Son of man, the Messianic Kingdom, demonology, resurrection, and eschatology. Surely the Christian story was developing out of this contemporary tradition?

The scrolls have revealed that the Essenes had a much-revered figure in their ancient past and is referred to in the *Damascus Document* of the Dead Sea Scrolls.

This obviously important priestly figure was their teacher, leader, and prophet, who would explain the allegory concealed within the scriptures and the Hebrew Bible.

The name of this being is never mentioned but he is referred to throughout, as the Teacher of Righteousness and for many respected scholars, and certainly for Alvar Ellegård in his book *Jesus: One Hundred Years Before Christ,* Century, 1999, he is a major character in the formation of the Christian myth. (Alvar Ellegård, 1919–2008, was a Swedish linguist and scholar. He was professor of English at the University of Gothenburg, and a member of the academic board of the Swedish National Encyclopedia.)

The texts tell us that the Teacher was leading the Essene sect around the late second century BCE and that he was considered as almost divine. As Vermes points out from his work on the Scrolls, "The Teacher of Righteousness, to whom God made known all the mysteries of the words of His servants and the prophets."

The Essenes, being a separated ascetic sect, did not appear to please the Jewish hierarchy and we learn that their leader and prophet, the Teacher, was taken by the authorities and as Vermes interprets the story, was probably put to death by the Jerusalem priests.

No names are mentioned but references are made to the "Wicked Priest" and the "Spouter of lies", and is suggested by Vermes as possibly being Jonathan Maccabaeus, High priest and King around 152–143 BCE.

The huge importance and reverence for the Teacher of Righteousness living on in the memory of the Essene Church as the Church of God, would have existed probably before the start of the first century CE.

Scholars such as Geza Vermes and Alvar Ellegård are under no doubt as to how great the influence of the Teacher was on the early history of the Essene groups. The question can be asked as to whether he was an actual historical figure or was he a creation of a later date, like the creation of the historical Jesus Christ? Of course, we cannot answer this. The scrolls certainly bring him alive as a living being but his actual existence really does not matter to us in our quest.

The fact that he was a pre-existent prophet, rooted firmly in the traditions and worship of the Church of God in Jerusalem, gives us good reason to look on him as another possibility in the identification of the figure perceived by Paul and the apostles of the Church of God in Jerusalem.

We can deduce that the Essenes and their associated sect of the Therapeutae were Gnostic thinkers. The Therapeutae in the Alexandria area, and most probably the Essenes, were also open to the influence of eastern mysticism; it is also likely that Buddhist philosophy would have been known to them.

The picture we can draw from the writings of the historians of the day, from the Dead Sea Scrolls and from archaeology, is that the Essenes and Therapeutae, and we may also include the Ebionites and the Nazoraeans to some degree, were an ascetic monastic sect, who set themselves apart from the main body of the Jews, i.e., the Pharisees and the Sadducees, and followed a unique way of life.

They were heavily influenced by the Book of Enoch, Jubilees and the Testaments of the Twelve Patriarchs, which was evident in the writings we have from the Scrolls. They were gnostic in their beliefs, looked at the scriptures in an allegorical way and changed their calendar from the Lunar to the Solar and were probably Sun worshippers.

They had mourned the loss of their great Teacher and prophet, the Teacher of Righteousness, his memory and reverence had lived on, right up to the time of Paul and his visions, and they expected their Teacher to send a messianic figure in these, their times of need.

Paul's revelation was shared by visions experienced by the senior leaders of the Jerusalem Church, and these pillars of the Church, Peter, James, and John are named as apostles but never referred to by Paul as Disciples.

This is a very important point: apostles are defined as missionaries or believers, whereas disciples and certainly the Disciples of Jesus, would be a far more personal and intimate companion. In his dealings with the Church, he never uses the word disciple.

Again, we must reiterate the fact, when Paul tells us about his meetings with these apostles, there is never any mention about a historical person of recent times. They tell him nothing of the life of Jesus. Like him, they relate to a Christ figure, now at God's side and speak absolutely nothing about the gospel figure we know so well. For me, this points to a pre-existent prophet from a distant time who they were all aware of and as a result of Paul's claims to have "seen" the resurrected prophet in his dream or vision, they concluded that the promised Messiah was imminent.

The Teacher had no name; it was secretly guarded and was never revealed in the scrolls. The name given to this prophet, this Teacher, the Redeemer, the Saviour, the Messiah, was Joshua, Yeshua, Lesous (Greek), or for us in the King James Bible, Jesus.

The Essenes in their Jerusalem Church, the Church of God, now had a messianic figure, which they believed would soon return and save them from the misery they had lived with for far too long.

This was the spiritual figure of the man who had died tragically more than a century ago and was probably still looked upon as a martyr and remembered in ritualistic practices. He now took on a massive importance.

Whichever way we look at this question of pre-existence, there is good scholarly support to back it up.

When I realized the possibilities of this theory, I was stunned by the factual information that was demonstrated to back it up and the conclusions I drew were that there was a figure of ancient times, who had been "seen" by Paul. I don't know whether that was the Essene Teacher of Righteousness or if it was the figure of the Old Testament Joshua or some other heavenly creation that could be moulded to fit the descriptions of the Old Testament prophecies.

Whichever it was, Paul had established the roots of the new Christian Church by revealing this prophet to the apostles of his Church of God and having called him Jesus the Christ, went on to evangelize in the Jewish diaspora, ultimately splitting with his original Essene brothers. He launched something that would be hijacked at a later date by the politically motivated bishops, only too pleased to oversee a complete history of the man. This was likely put together by the Greek scholars, who composed the gospel stories more than a generation later than when Paul's imagination produced the spiritual Messiah.

Some of the Essenes were quick to take up the good news that Paul brought to them and accepted the Jesus figure as the Christ or Messiah. Some were not so enthusiastic. Paul was turning the expected leader into something of a divine super-being and he was opening up the faith to the Gentiles who would not have to live by Jewish Law. We read in Paul's epistles about the problems he faced with the pillars of the Jerusalem Church and how eventually, Peter carried on the Church of God in Jerusalem. Peter appealed to the Jews, while Paul turned his evangelization to the diaspora and the Gentiles, who readily accepted his new religion of forgiveness and eternal life via faith in the Christ, with some enthusiasm.

Many of the Essenes in the diaspora took up the faith in the Jesus Messiah, too, and maintained their beliefs, writings and scriptures, as well as their mystery laden philosophy; the new Christianity emerged from the mix.

Scholars have noted how early Christianity and the Essene church were very similar, and certainly both used the Book of Enoch and its supernatural teachings as an important scriptural text. It was the fusion of the two that resulted in today's Christian Church.

However, the views of that very early Christian Church, with foundations deeply rooted in Essenism, were very different in regard to the way they perceived their Jesus.

The teaching of Christianity of early beginnings and that which developed in the second century, were very different belief structures.

This early faith was undoubtedly immersed in Gnostic ideas. You remember what we said at the outset about Gnosticism and their ideas about spiritual beings and visions? This is amply demonstrated by Paul not only in his revelations via visions but also in his language. Paul's Letter to the Ephesians is often quoted as having heavy gnostic overtones.

"[T]he most Gnostically oriented of the Paulines: Ephesians" (Alvar Ellegård, *Jesus: One Hundred Years Before Christ. A study in Creative Mythology*, Overlook Press, 2002).

Although the Essenes did not share a totally Gnostic outlook with Gnostics of the time, the spirituality of their beliefs was probably enough to attract many to their cause and the Essenes of the diaspora together with their associated Therapeutae, would possibly have had far more Gnostic ways about them than their parent group at the Jerusalem Church. And of course, it was this parent church, the Jerusalem Church of God, which disappeared completely at the time of the destruction of the city and the Temple in 70 CE, as did all traces of the Essene communities. The Qumran community were probably anticipating this destruction and hid their precious history, the Scrolls, for safekeeping in the hill caves on the shores of the Dead Sea.

The developing Jesus cult based on the history of a pre-existent superhero in the distant past of the Jewish sect of Essenes and Therapeutae was now being moulded into a first-century Christ or Messiah, but he remained firmly in the world of spirit. He was not walking amongst them and nobody thought that he had for maybe a hundred or possibly, several hundreds of years.

This was very much a world of Gnostic belief.

It cannot be overstated that the lack of historical detail in the Letters of Paul, the starting point for the foundation of the New Testament, is something that should be examined critically. Equally, the very early writings in the New Testament that include Peter and James, are similarly apparently totally ignorant of any elements of Jesus as a man. Not only can we relate to early New Testament writings but early scriptures outside of the Canon also show not a hint of any detail to describe a man who worked miracles and lived in Galilee, died and resurrected around the year 30 CE.

It is truly incredible and not really appreciated by most Bible readers, that the first-century writers, and to that we can add Paul, Peter, James, and Jude, show absolutely no knowledge of the life story of the Jesus figure, who suddenly comes to life in a historical sense, in the gospels of Mark, Matthew, Luke and John. None of them place their Saviour in the very recent past.

There is a reason for this and hopefully, I have been able to make some suggestions that make sense, when the whole story is looked upon with the eyes of the spiritual Gnostics who lived by visions and saw their Messiah as only a spirit.

Probably, Paul was not fully Gnostic in his philosophy, but

he certainly showed many of the common traits. His Jesus was taken up by the diaspora Jews and eventually the Gentiles who knew that their Jesus was still in Heaven at the side of God and would soon come to earth and be amongst them at the End Times and the Day of Judgement. They simply didn't know about Mary and Joseph and the stable story. It had not yet been created.

We will look a bit more at this Gnostic milieu that saw the development of the myth but before we do, let's look at some of the firm, concrete evidence that proves unequivocally that Jesus the Christ lived the life of a man in Galilee at the time designated by the four gospels.

Chapter 10

What Evidence?

Archaeologists are the first to admit that the evidence of absence does not prove the absence of evidence and so it is with our search for information from independent sources for some substantial historical evidence for the existence of Jesus Christ.

Here is a man who ticked all the boxes to make the front page on every historical text that would have been written from the mid-thirties of the first century CE onwards.

A man genuinely born to a virgin mother by the magic of a Jewish God. A man who was declared to be the Son of that God, and a man who became God on earth.

He developed into a worker of wondrous deeds, he raised dead people back to life, he did anything that the Greek and Egyptian gods had done before him and he did it better, he said profound things and even when alone, fighting the temptations of Satan, his words were recorded for posterity, by whom we do not know.

He led an incredibly similar life to some of his Greek and Persian predecessors, not to mention the Egyptian, Buddhist and Indian deities.

He died a tragic and cruel death on the cross, stake or tree and like many of his forebears, came back to life after three days and was seen by many people, including five hundred apostles who apparently said very little about their meeting. In fact, they said nothing.

At the time of the crucifixion there was a truly incredible happening that the whole of the empire would have spoken of. The ground was split apart, and the bodies of the dead came back to life and were even recorded in the Gospel of Matthew as going into town where they met friends and family.

He was seen by women after his resurrection, and it is at this point that the stories become a little contradictory. The story goes on in a way that you are familiar with because of what we have been told.

None of this fantastic detail was ever recorded by any scribes or contemporary historians outside of the pages of the four gospels and the Acts of the Apostles.

Surely, the zombie story alone with bodies leaping out of the ground, should have made an impression on someone?

Why were the five hundred witnesses never mentioned again after Paul tells us about their visions? Who were they? Even more important, when was it? Did they mention the fact that they had seen a dead man come back to life and he was the Son of God? Five hundred witnesses to the raised Jesus, not mentioned even by the gospel scribes.

Just think about some of the miraculous happenings that would have stunned the people of the day. Here is a man who fed thousands of people with two fishes and the same man was able to calm storms, just like other ancient gods and could even walk on water. Now, the people of the time were, in so many ways very different to us in their world view, but even if they saw somebody skimming across the waves without getting wet, then they would be more than a little surprised.

I am honestly not trying to be facetious in saying these things, but they are points which must be raised if we are to come to any conclusions about the historicity of the Jesus godman.

If these things happened, they would have been truly stupendous happenings of the day. The fact that the gospels record them is not good enough for our quest, because it's those very gospels which are at issue. Of course, the gospel writers will write these things because that is what fitted the requirements of the time.

Surely, some or all these remarkable events would have been recorded by someone other than the gospel creators? We have already established that the early Testament writers of Paul, Peter, James, and non-Canonical writers, like Clement of Rome and the writer of the Pastor of Hermes, plus so many others, do not mention a single word of this. True, they do mention a crucifixion and a resurrection but make it absolutely clear that they do not intend to mention a time or place, or whether that resurrection was purely spiritual as they imply or was it a physical coming back to life as the gospel writers would have us believe.

There were other very well-known historians at the time of the supposed Jesus story who were plying their trade during the fantastic goings on of the first century.

It's very important to be in touch with the works of some of these ancient scribes, as it is the usual argument put forward by the Christian apologists who will try to hang onto any tiny piece of possible evidence that might give some credibility to a human being who came to earth as God and man.

We must look at what was written at the time, or soon after, by the great historians Philo the Jew, Josephus, Suetonius, and Tacitus.

Philo, who was an Alexandrian Jewish philosopher and historian, lived between the years of 20 BCE–45 CE (approx.), a perfect time to be an actual witness to the incredible events.

Philo, you may remember, was the writer who told us about the Essenes and their mystical relatives the Therapeutae. He was very interested in Hellenistic philosophy and Jewish belief. His influence on early Christianity and his concept of a Logos, a sort of mediator between God and man, has been commented upon by scholars. But what of his comments at the time regarding the miraculous events in Palestine? Well, he did not have very much to say about the Son of God who was walking around at the same time as him. In fact, in none of the works we have from Philo does he mention Jesus. He never mentions him or his works, or the zombies, or the fish miracle; nothing at all.

It is simply not conceivable that Philo would have ignored these events if he had known about them. Did he know? How could he not if they had actually happened?

The great Jewish historian Philo who lived at the time of the birth, death and resurrection of Jesus does not make a single mention of him.

Josephus (38–100 CE) was one of the most famous, if not *the* most famous, of historians of the late first century.

His works *The History of the Jewish War* and *Jewish Antiquities* are hailed as comprehensive records of many of the important and not so important events of the times.

In his work *The History of the Jewish War* he makes no mention of Christians or Christianity, even though the religion was supposedly developing rapidly around the Roman Empire at the time of his writing. It had obviously made little impression.

In his volume *Jewish Antiquities* there is a significant paragraph, which appears almost out of the blue, not in any chronological sequence and does not seem to fit where it is placed. This passage is treasured by those who profess the historicity of Jesus as a man, as it is almost the only piece of debatable reference material they can relate to.

The passage reads,

Now, about this time, Jesus, a wise man, if it be lawful to call him a man, for he was a doer of wonderful works, a teacher of such men as receive the truth with pleasure. He drew over to him both many of the Jews and many of the Gentiles. He was the Christ, and when Pilate at the suggestion of the principal men amongst us, had condemned him to the cross, those that loved him at the first did not forsake him, for he appeared to them alive again the third day, as the divine prophets had foretold these and ten thousand other wonderful things concerning him, and the tribe of Christians, so named after him, are not extinct at this day.

(The Works of Flavius Josephus, Whiston's Translation, Revised, with Topographical Notes, *Antiquities of the Jews, the Jewish War, and Against Apion*, Volumes 1–5 (complete), first editions, 1883)

There it is! Almost the whole life story neatly packaged in one paragraph and one paragraph that does not relate to the previous or the one that followed. It is almost universally rejected as a forgery of possibly the fourth century CE.

The paragraph is known as the *Testimonium Flavianum* and is repeated endlessly by Christian apologists desperate to make an historical point.

What immediately jumps out is that Josephus was a Jew and as a Jew, not a Christian, he would not announce the arrival of the Christ or Messiah unless he agreed with that fact. As a Jew, for him, Jesus was not the Messiah.

The English biblical scholar Rev. Sabine Baring-Gould, in a piece of work from 1874, writes scathingly, "One maybe, perhaps be accused of killing dead birds, if one examines and discredits the passage."

Amazingly, the Church fathers, such as Justin Martyr, Tertullian, Clement of Alexandria, and Origen, never use the passage in their arguments against the detractors they seemed to battle with on a regular basis.

Had they have known of this perfect piece of potted history they would surely have used it in their writings.

Certainly, Justin Martyr could have made good use of this paragraph when he tells us of his Dialogue with Trypho the Jew.

Written in approximately 150 CE, the Church father, Justin Martyr is discussing philosophy and the nature of Jesus Christ as the Christian Saviour. Trypho rejects the story of Jesus completely and says, in the now famous paragraph, "But Christ, if he has indeed been born and exists anywhere, is unknown and does not even know himself and has no power until Elias come and make him manifest to all. And you, having accepted a groundless report, invent a Christ for yourselves and for his sake are inconsiderately perishing."

So here we have an educated Jew accusing Justin Martyr of inventing the Jesus story and telling him that he doubts that Jesus ever existed.

Trypho would have been very aware of the works of Josephus and had Justin Martyr been aware of the paragraph relating to Jesus the man, he would certainly have used it.

Was Trypho's opinion typical of educated Jews at the time? Was it common for them to see the Jesus story as an invention from something that was never meant to be historical?

Many Christian scholars reluctantly agree that the paragraph inserted into the pages of Josephus is a forgery of a later date and that it was first brought to life by the totally unreliable church propagandist Eusebius in the fourth century CE. It is he who shoulders the accusations of guilt in some sections of the academic world.

There must be some valid historical document that gives some firm confirmation to the arguments put forward by Christian scholars.

Well, not only did our friend Josephus supposedly write that wonderful piece of history relating to Jesus but he also added another piece which tells us about James his brother.

This unfortunately is another piece of work viewed in many quarters with a critical eye.

It tells the story of the death of James and refers to him as the brother of Jesus; but this vague reference does not stand up when you consider that all members of the Church of God were related to as Brothers and if Josephus was aware that this James was the brother of Christ, then he would, based on his previous mention of Jesus, have realized that he was talking about God's brother.

Surely God's brother would merit a lot more information than something so vague that many scholars cannot come to any firm decision on the validity or meaning of this passage.

If Josephus was genuinely aware of James, the brother of Jesus Christ, why did he not seem to have any idea at all about the rest of the group who supposedly played a massive part in the history of the day. Why no mention of Peter the Rock of the Church? Why no mention of Paul? Nothing about the man that started the ball rolling and, of course, there was not a word about the five hundred people who witnessed the risen body of Jesus, three days after his death. Surely, that would be worth a mention?

Are the few brief references to Jesus in the Josephus later forgeries, interpolations of scribes desperate to add something to a history sadly lacking, or were they oral traditions that were beginning to develop at the time of Josephus' writing?

For a Christ figure of such magnitude and importance and life story so fantastic, I think you'll agree that the evidence does look a little sparse?

A final thought on that. If the James he refers to is the James of the New Testament as in the Letter of James, it is quite possible that that letter was written by the apostle James, who was one of the leaders of the Church of God, according to Paul, and as such was probably quite a learned man. Hence, the extremely good Greek in which the letter is written. The Disciple James, i.e., someone who lived closely to Jesus at the time of his sojourn on earth, would have been an illiterate fisherman, unable to write such excellent prose.

So, if he really is the apostle James, who met Paul, and walked about with Peter, why does he not refer to himself as the Brother of Christ, that is to say, God's Brother? Even if it was written by someone other than the real James, apostle, and pillar of the Church, why does he not refer to himself as the Brother of Jesus?

Paul refers to the Lord's brother but of course this almost certainly means an apostle serving God, as the God of the Old Testament is looked upon as the Lord.

In the gospels, we do read about Jesus and his family but they seem to play a very minor part in his life story. If one of those brothers was indeed James, who was a blood relative, and it was he who went on to be such a major player in the Church of God, then I suspect the gospel writers would have given him far more importance.

If you were compiling a gospel and wanted some extra ammunition to bolster the story, surely to mention that the Church leader, James the Apostle, was the actual blood brother of the supernatural Christ, would be an absolute must. Luke, when he speaks of James, never mentions this startling fact.

The Catholic Church does not go along with this Brother of Jesus theory, and I don't think I do either, but perhaps for different reasons.

It strikes me that the fact that we have to even debate the existence of a living Jesus the man, means in itself that there is something very wrong with the claims of the historicists. Such a massive happening as the Jewish God Yahweh sending a supernatural human to earth and having a few brothers, too, would have left far more evidence than we are able to muster.

Nevertheless, we will push on and see what else can point to absolute proof of the supernatural appearance of the godman Yeshua.

We are now running short of any convincing source material to relate to outside the pages of the gospels.

There is, however, another oft quoted reference used by apologists when the arguments are beginning to look a bit thin.

This involves the writing of Tacitus.

Tacitus was a Roman historian and lived around the time 55–117 CE. He is remembered for *The Annals of Imperial Rome* and *The Histories*. It is in *The Annals* that we hear about the Emperor

Nero who not too pleased about the fire in Rome, decided to blame it on the Christians. Oddly enough, the word Christian at this time was still not being used.

The reference in *Annals* goes on to tell us that this bunch of arsonists were followers of one Christus; he then goes on to tell the story of his death via Pontius Pilate.

Tacitus relates that there were vast numbers of these Christians in Rome at that time, but history has demonstrated that there were no vast numbers anywhere at such an early date.

It certainly appears that Tacitus had picked up his information from the new Christians of his day and he was merely repeating what he was being told from the developing life story being created around him.

Many scholars have discussed this passage from Tacitus and the general opinion is that it carries little or no weight in proving the existence of Jesus the man.

Readers should look at the works of D.M. Murdock and Herbert Cutner for more on this subject.

Finally, another of the Roman historians, Suetonius (circa 69–122 CE), in his work *Life of Claudius*, tells us that there were Jews constantly rioting in Rome at the suggestion of a person called Chrestus, who could be anybody.

As far as contemporary historical evidence for the man Jesus goes, that is about it.

There is nothing written in the first century CE outside the four gospels that gives any indication of real substance that a man called Jesus lived and performed those wondrous deeds we hear about from later writers.

As I said in an earlier chapter, even the dates of the four main gospels of the New Testament are of an uncertain date. Ellegård suggests, with good evidence, that none of them were written until much later than has been accepted in the past.

Christian scholars want an early date to give more credibility to the argument that there was an oral tradition carried on after the death on the cross, ultimately being written down in the gospels, at a date as early as they could get away with.

The evidence we have therefore, for confirmation of a living, historical man called Jesus, who lived in Palestine in the early years of the first century, outside the gospels of Matthew, Mark, Luke, and John, can be summed up as follows:

Josephus' account in *Antiquities*, the Jesus paragraph, considered by virtually all scholars to be a forgery and that includes some Catholic scholars. The mention in Josephus of James, the Brother of Jesus. Again, considered by most scholars to be totally unreliable and a probable interpolation of a later date. There is simply no firm evidence anywhere to say that James was a blood brother of God on earth.

Tacitus and his reports about Christians causing trouble for Nero. It seems that Tacitus' accounts of Christians suffering under Nero do not stand up to historical examination. He reports on torture and executions in Rome around 64 CE and yet the Book of Acts tells us that at the same time Paul was evangelizing quite freely, with "no man forbidding him". Even our friend Tertullian never used this stuff in his determined efforts to prove the Christian cause.

In his passage in *Annals*, Tacitus refers only to Christus not Jesus of Nazareth and like the other texts quoted, is seen as very suspect and not worth very much as a confirmation of history. He was picking up on the mythical story as it developed at the time.

Why do we have no concrete, reliable references in history written by independent historians of the time, or indeed any archaeology, to back up the story as provided by the creators of the gospels?

We have absolutely no firm evidence from any of these non-Christian writers, who themselves had no particular religious point to prove. It looks, quite simply, that they, like the writers of the early scriptures and certainly the apostle Paul, had no knowledge of a living Jesus in the early years of the century. We are looking at the probability of a pre-existent Yeshua or Teacher, who was resurrected by Paul's visions and those of the Church leaders.

I cannot believe, and I suspect that neither can you, that some of the most incredible happenings ever to happen on earth were not recorded by the educated historians of the day.

The American writer and biblical critic John E. Remsburg (1848–1919) in *The Christ* lists forty-two historians and writers who lived during or within a hundred years of the life of Jesus, not one of whom ever mention him (Taken from an essay of Marshall J. Gauvin, "Did Jesus Christ Really Live?", 1922).

Like most people, I never even knew about the passage in Matthew (27:50), which when I read it, astounded me.

How could the ground split open and the long since dead leap out of their graves and saunter quite casually into town, go to meet their relatives and probably live again and die another death at a later day?

This was not recorded by anybody at all except Matthew. Did it happen? Of course not.

Incredible supernatural events supposedly witnessed by thousands, such as the miracle of the fishes and loaves, did not merit one word of historical reference from an independent writer around at the time.

If Philo or Josephus had known about these slightly out of the ordinary events, or the other forty historians mentioned by Remsburg, I am certain they would have written volumes on the godman Jesus.

Did they not even know about Paul and the huge upheaval caused by the resurrected Messiah around the years 30–33 CE? No, they did not.

Like I said many pages back, without a knowledge of those elements of Greek, Egyptian, Roman, and Persian history, and an ability to examine first-century Christianity with an analytical eye, the Jesus story would be accepted in every way and it was.

Now you, like me, have a bit more of an insight into those supposed histories of the gospels, it starts to look like a very much weaker foundation that they base their truths on. Maybe you do not agree, but the fact remains that the material we are discovering in the pages of this book is very real: the doubts about His historicity are based on good scholarship and the Mythicist Theory in my opinion is undoubtedly gaining ground. The historical evidence for Jesus the man is less than weak, and faith alone is certainly not enough to maintain the validity of the gospels. History does not work like that.

Chapter 11

The Word of God or Men?

The Old Testament, according to most modern Jewish scholars, was never meant to be read as a history book. The incredibly supernatural stories immersed in myth and magic and number symbolism are to be taken as allegories and symbolic in their meaning.

Only a fanatical believer could believe the story of Adam and Eve, the Garden of Eden, and the Great Flood, with Noah saving the day with his Ark. Even this was surrounded by number symbolism, as we are given the exact dimensions that the vessel should conform to; numbers which conceal a far deeper significance.

Do you believe what the writer of 2 Kings 2:11 tells us when we hear that Elijah the prophet made his exit in such grand style? Horses of fire and a chariot of flames came down from the sky and he hops in and takes off into a better place, at one with Yahweh the sky God.

He does turn up again, in the words of Mark 9:4, in the pages of the New Testament, where he and his friend Moses appear with Jesus as he turns into a bright light in his transfiguration.

It is all nonsense as a story of history but symbolically, it represents other things, as do so many of the elements of the Old Testament.

The well-known story of the Suffering Servant in Isaiah 53 has been looked upon as having many allegorical meanings, with many scholars believing that it refers to the nation of Israel itself.

Nothing is the way it appears. We mentioned earlier the accounts of Abraham, Moses and the other great patriarchs of the ancient Hebrews. None of these characters have any foundations in history. No confirmation of their existence outside the pages of the Bible or indeed any archaeological evidence can verify their historical deeds.

At least in Egypt we do have the pyramid hieroglyphs that tell the life stories of their great pharaohs but realistically, the history of the heroes of very early Judaism is more than sparse, it's non-existent.

The myths of the Hebrew Bible, the Old Testament, are creations, a way of developing a deeply spiritual, yet allegorical history that probably never happened.

It would be ridiculous to claim that there is no history at all in the Old Testament, of course there is. The places mentioned, the stories of the Hebrews in exile, their time in Egypt, almost certainly do have general aspects of historical accuracy but to talk in such detail about the wonderful deeds of a Moses figure, and the others, is without foundation.

Archaeology is rapidly changing the way we see so many things, which for years were taken as biblical truths.

The monotheistic nature of early Jewish religious history is now under serious doubt. It was taken for granted that there was only one true God of Israel, the great tribal God Yahweh, a male God with no evidence of a female consort, in sharp contrast to other ancient deities.

For a long time now archaeologists have been finding evidence that this is probably not true at all.

Female figurines have been excavated at several sites for many years and now, at last, it seems that the unutterable can be spoken.

There is a strong body of opinion that the God Yahweh was associated with the female figure of Asherah, originally the wife of El in Ugaritic mythology and appears alongside Baal, the god of the Canaanites, who is mentioned in the Hebrew Bible, certainly in Books 1 and 2 of Kings, but in a way that does not imply a relationship with their God.

Baal worship is also mentioned in the Book of Judges 8:33, where the writer bemoans the fact that the Israelites had gone over to the other side. If so, the ancient memories of Baal worship would never be totally wiped out.

The developing Hebrew Jewish religious system would have been heavily influenced by the many goddess cults of the time and for them not to have been in some way attracted to them, is not realistic.

The goddess culture has and still is being suppressed by the male-dominated religious leadership, who dogmatically refuse to accept the growing evidence, which in the present day, even calls Asherah the Wife of God!

The history created by those ancient Hebrew scribes was meant to give a past and a future to the long-suffering people. They created their all-powerful God, Yahweh, a jealous and often cruel God. Although Yahweh was their one true God, it seems that other gods were being worshipped at the same time!

If this is true then the possibility of the consort Asherah does not look so unlikely.

If you look at Ezekiel 8:14 there is a remarkable passage that tells of women at the Temple weeping for their god Tammuz. "Then He brought me to the door of the gate of the Lord's house, which was towards the north and behold, there sat the women weeping for Tammuz."

Tammuz was the Babylonian god that represented the Osiris Isis legend as we described earlier, and he was the archetypal dying and resurrecting vegetation god or Sun god which we have come to expect. He had a female consort called Ishtar, who would have been well known to the people in the Temple of Jerusalem. You can see how quickly this gets all a bit complicated! Many Bible readers still cannot accept this passage in Ezekiel as the implications are very far reaching; as in dying and resurrecting gods.

The point is that what we are reading in our Bible is not

meant to be taken as historical fact. There is a lot more going on that needs a far deeper understanding.

We should bear in mind that those created mythologies and allegories which gave credibility to the past and future of the developing nation, were the very myths and prophecies which were scrutinized by the much later gospel writers who used them to give absolute confirmation to the Jesus Christ figure and his life story, invented by the New Testament compilers several hundred years later.

So much of the Jesus story leaps out of the Hebrew Bible, which in itself would give total credibility to the myth because prophecies in the Septuagint, Old Testament in Greek, were not just prophecies, they were absolute truths, and they would come to pass and come to pass they did: the gospel creators made sure of that.

It is interesting to look at some of the Messianic prophecies and where they appeared in the New Testament.

The virgin birth is prophesied. (Isaiah7:14 and Matthew 1:21)

Birth in Bethlehem. (Micah 5:2 and Matthew 2:1)

Travels into Egypt. (Hosea 11:1 and Matthew 2:14)

Herod kills the children. (Jeremiah 31:15 and Matthew 2:16)

Able to perform miraculous deeds. (Isaiah 35:5 and Matthew 9:35)

Enter Jerusalem on donkey. (Zechariah 9:9 and Matthew 21:4)

Betrayed by a close associate. (Psalm 41:9 and Luke 22:3)

Thirty pieces of silver. (Zechariah 11:12 and Matthew 26:14)

Crucified with criminals. (Isaiah 53:12 and Matthew 27:38)

Given vinegar to drink. (Psalm 69:21 and Matthew 27:34)

Rise from death. (Psalm 16:10 and Acts 2:31)

Cast lots for his clothes. (Psalm 22:18 and John 19:23)

And, so, they go on. There are dozens of them. Wonderful fanciful prophecies which if fulfilled would create the ultimate divine being, and that is exactly what they did, they created the

Messiah Jesus Christ and made sure that the prophecies were fulfilled in the life they created for Him.

Christians sometimes comment that they find it odd that the stories of the Old Testament are found in the same book as the stories of Jesus and his ministry in Palestine. They often do not see the links between a purely Jewish story book and the later stories of the Christian Messiah. The two are irrevocably linked and the New Testament would not have happened without the guidelines of the Old Testament.

The wildly supernatural stories of the Old Testament writers are so obviously not to be taken as real events, although many people still do: Flaming chariots, parting of the seas, apocalyptic floods, serpents tempting people, and folk living to the ripe old age of many hundreds of years are simply the way stories were told in those days. They were symbolic allegories, with a bit of colour for effect.

We do not know who wrote them, or when, but scholars suggest a date as early as the thirteenth century BCE for the oldest material, which is embedded in the books of the current Hebrew Bible and which reached their current form at various dates between the fifth century BCE and the second century BCE (*Bible: Growth of Literature*, Encyclopaedia Americana, Grolier, Online).

The Hebrew Bible, the Old Testament, was translated into Greek around the years 275–100 BCE, when it was known as the Septuagint. It is suggested that the name, which implies the number seven, came from the fact that seventy Jewish scholars were chosen to translate the Law of Moses into Greek so that it could be included at the great library of Alexandria (*Letter of Aristeas*).

As you would expect, there is much scholarly debate about these dates and the original content.

Nothing is certain about any of the creative writing in the Old Testament, but it certainly gave a developing culture its solid historical foundations, which has carried through, virtually unchanged, to the present day.

I should mention that the ancient biblical texts found amongst the codices of the Dead Sea Scrolls seem to be very similar textually to what we read today.

I still find it hard to believe that people can, even today, be convinced that the written word is the word of God and all the wonderful myth makers, who composed the stories of the God Yahweh making the earth in seven days, and the Garden of Eden tale we read about, is actual history, recorded for us from scribes at the time.

These beliefs, like the rest of it, were created for simple folk to give an explanation to life and for the more profound, hidden symbolism in name and number, that carried a more spiritual message.

I wonder how many Church ministers today, do in their heart, really believe the more bizarre side of so many of those stories? There is a chapter in Judges 8:30 that casually mentions Gideon having seventy sons. That is some going. Possible, but who was counting them?

And then in 2 Chronicles 1:7, the scribe recording the event, tells us "That night, God appeared to Solomon and said ..." God quite casually appears and has a conversation. If you ever read what happens to the poor unfortunate chap Job, I think you, like me, will see the Old Testament for what it is: a great story book.

I believe the New Testament is a truly wonderful piece of literature. I say that with genuine admiration for the writers who created such a masterpiece of storytelling, encompassing all the wisdom and spiritual guidance that we see from any of the gospels.

It probably is one of the greatest spiritual books ever written; but is not to be looked upon as a book of ancient history.

Scholars readily admit that the four gospels are not to be read as accurate events in history, and even the Christian defender

Origen, in the third century, admits that not everything you read in the scriptures is to be looked at as factual.

"Origen points out, there are so many discrepancies in the accounts presented by the gospels, that one must admit that their truth does not lie in their literal sense" (John Behr, *The Way to Nicaea*, p. 177. St Vladimir's Seminary Press, 2001).

Even as early as the time of Origen (185–254 CE), the educated commentators of the day were fully aware of the allegorical nature of the scriptures. They knew the Bible was the creation of inspired men and not a divine creation.

The Bible is a human product, not a divine product.

The Bible is not to be interpreted literally, factually and absolutely. Its language is often metaphorical, and its primary concern is not factual reporting. Its laws and ethical teaching are not absolutes relevant to all times and places but are the product of those ancient communities and address their time and place. This does not mean that its laws and ethics are irrelevant to our time. But they cannot be simply transferred to the twenty-first century.

(*Conversations with Scripture: The Gospel of Mark*, Anglican Association of Biblical Scholars, Morehouse Publishing, 2009)

The fact is, we know virtually nothing about the history of the gospels. We do not know who wrote them and the names allocated to them, like Mark or Matthew, mean nothing. The gospels are named according to Mark and Matthew, not written by them.

We most certainly do not know when they were written. I keep reminding you that gospel dating is not an accurate science and anything between the years of 70 CE and 140 CE is open to debate, with a good argument having been made by some scholars for the writings to have come out of the second century CE.

As to where they were written, almost universally, it is agreed that they were written in the diaspora with probably Alexandria playing a major role. They were written in good Greek from an educated hand and not in the Aramaic of the time and place of Jesus. Nobody of any scholastic standing believes that anything in the New Testament is written by any of the disciples of Jesus, nor were they written by any eyewitnesses to the supposed historical events. Apologists will have us believe that they were compilations of memories passed on by oral tradition and as such were passed on accurately, without change for decades.

Most would agree, though several these days do not, that Mark is the oldest of the four, followed by Matthew, Luke and then John.

The first three are known collectively as the Synoptic gospels, because of their similarities.

Mark may possibly have been the first gospel, which was expanded upon by Matthew and Luke, who added a little more meat to the bones.

The Gospel of Mark does not mention a birth narrative, or in its original form, a full resurrection story and originally ended at chapter 16:8. Later, more was added to the story creating another twelve verses.

Serious questions must be answered by the omissions and indeed the additions.

Did Mark even know about a virgin birth at the time of writing, or was this an invention of Matthew for more effect? The resurrection account opens up even more problems, but these subjects could fill a book on its own and it is not possible to study the full origins of the Gospel of Mark here, but suffice to say, I am very suspicious about why Mark was added to at a later date. This is something that even the Bible (NRSV) adds as a comment at the point of the original ending 16:8. In the shorter ending there is no resurrection story with witnesses, like Mary

Magdalene. That was added on later.

Never forget that Paul should precede the four gospels, as his writings are accepted as the earliest of the Testament writings. Of course, he does not appear in the correct place, because by the time you read the Letters of Paul, you have already acquired a full life story of the man, which fits in nicely with the total lack of earthly detail in Paul. You simply do not notice. You take for granted that Paul knew what you know. The facts seem to clearly point to the reality that he didn't know.

The Christ of Paul, Peter and James, and indeed some of the other very early scriptures not in the Canon, seem to relate to a very different Jesus figure to that of the gospels.

One is a distinctly spiritual being displaying Gnostic characteristics, while the gospel Jesus is suddenly a man of real history with fantastic detail to support his reality. In the gospels themselves there is further reason to see a different Jesus in the Gospel of John than in the Synoptics.

The Jesus of John is a distinctly Gnostic spiritual being who seems to be God himself. The writer is made to make Jesus a little less Gnostic by certain elements in the story that take away that docetic idea that the Gnostics taught. You remember, Docetism was the philosophy that Jesus only appeared to be a man. In fact, he was pure spirit.

Remarkably, we have no mention or reference to the Synoptic gospels or their names of Mark, Matthew and Luke until as late as 190 CE, when the ever-present Irenaeus relates to them.

In fact, we do not even know when the four gospels were lumped together under the heading of the Canonical gospels, or why these four from dozens of scriptures available at the time were chosen. Supposedly it was Irenaeus, again, who decided that there could be neither more nor less than four gospels, just as there are four points of the compass (Irenaeus, *Adv. Haer.*, 3:11).

Of those other available scriptures, many would have been

of a Gnostic nature and would therefore be heresy to the Father Irenaeus: he chose the ones that fitted the political bill.

As a piece of history, these texts, written maybe generations after the supposed happenings, and in a language and place that distanced them even further from the original events, makes them very weak as evidence of a living man. Creations based on myth would not be contradicted because there were no living memories still around to make the point!

We don't even have the original words for any of these gospel accounts. What we read has been copied many, many times from the original accounts of the second century, by the hands of Christian monks who were not averse to tampering with anything they did not understand or agree with.

All scholars agree that forgeries, interpolations, alterations, omissions and additions are inevitable during the centuries of copying that took place and I think I hear that song coming on again "The things that you're liable, to read in the Bible, it ain't necessarily so."

The original texts have long since disappeared and the oldest we have is a compilation from hundreds of years later. The Codex Sinaiticus, from the fourth century, displays big differences to the subsequent bibles that followed, and it is here that we see how the Gospel of Mark has been tampered with, with Jesus Christ not appearing as the living Saviour after the resurrection.

That tampering was a common practice is upheld by all serious scholars and not just tampering but downright forgeries, too, were common.

The English historian Rev. John Allen Giles (1808–1884), made the point that,

"There can be no doubt that there were great numbers of books then written with no other view than to deceive."

Rev. William Robertson Smith (1846–1894), Professor of Arabic and a fellow of Christ's College, Cambridge, a respected historian, wrote that during the evolution of the early Christian Church "there was an enormous floating mass of spurious literature created to suit party views."

How much of this spurious and deceptive literature was included in the New Testament?

Although the three synoptic gospels are meant to be similar and do relate to each other, there are huge discrepancies demonstrated which bring into question the historical value of anything that is written.

Most scholars question the value of the lineage of Jesus, drawn up by Matthew and then in the Gospel of Luke. They differ almost completely from start to finish and are a record of the lineage of his father, Joseph. It may be churlish to comment that God is the father of Jesus.

I suspect that there is more going on in the actual numbers of generations quoted by the gospel writers here and those numbers may have a deeper significance, as we shall see later. I think the writers were aware of their contradictions in the lineage. There may be something more profound going on in the numbers of the generations. Numbers were critically important in Bible speak; something most scholars of Divinity have been unaware of for far too long.

The birth criteria have caused huge problems for the early scribes. Mark was clever, he did not even want to get involved in this myth making. Matthew and Luke have a stable scene almost ten years apart. A big difference if the story was an accurate account of a massive event.

History does not record the census that took Mary and Joseph on their memorable journey, and incredibly it has been noted that Nazareth, the town where they lived, probably never even existed at that time. No historical or archaeological evidence exists to attest to its existence at the time of Jesus.

"We cannot perhaps venture to assert positively that there was a city of Nazareth in Jesus' time" (*Encyclopaedia Biblica*).

The contradictions and discrepancies really do make one ask some searching questions.

How can the birth stories be so different and even non-existent, what happened to Jesus in all those years before he appeared as a man in Galilee? Why is it only Luke who makes a fleeting mention of the young God involving himself with the elders at the Temple?

Why does John place the money lenders story at a different time in the ministry of Jesus. The other three saw it as a far more important happening and at a different time, too.

Like the Old Testament, the people who put the gospel stories together were not relating history; they never meant to. They were writing fanciful creations which gave life and meaning, in a way easily understood by the non-too literate masses, to a life story of a man who simply had to be seen as a real earthly being. It is often said Jesus did not create the Church, it was the Church that created Jesus.

If there ever was a real man called Jesus, a man who preached a decent way of life and had probably learned some Egyptian mysticism that impressed the crowds in the town, then he left absolutely no mark on the pages of contemporary history. He was never a son of a tribal god and he disappeared from the history of his time without anyone bothering to record his presence. The gospel writers certainly changed that.

But, with the evidence at hand, I maintain a position that Jesus Christ the man, was the invention of the learned Greeks who wrote the wonderful verses of literature that have stayed with us for two thousand years. Remember, those words of divine wisdom were not written by the pen held in a celestial hand stretching down from heaven and composing the works of Matthew, Mark, Luke and John: they were created by men, real humans who had a purpose in mind. They came from a different time when storytelling and history were looked at in a different way and those early Christian writers, as we have demonstrated, were not averse to a bit of textual fiddling to make their version of events fit the political necessities of the day!

Who was it that made the creation of the gospels so necessary and, indeed, why was it necessary to create a life story for a man, who until then, had been a purely spiritual being in the minds and souls of those early Christians who revered his memory, and looked upon him as their Saviour?

An interesting question!

To answer that, we should reflect on the situation that was prevalent before the gospels were created.

You remember we established the probability that the Jesus Christ figure, worshipped in the Essene Church of God at the time of Paul's vision, was a pre-existent saviour figure, known to the faithful from a long time back in history.

This spiritual Saviour, Yeshua, Jesus, Joshua, became their expected Messiah. It was not long before the gnostic thinkers of the time took up the figure of the now quite well-known Christ, (Christ meaning spirit) and developed their mystical thinking and religious journey to find their God within by using Jesus as their teacher and leader.

The Gnostic writers developed their own stories of their spiritual teacher and were happy to commune with Him in their own spiritual way.

Some of the Gnostics would admit that there may have been an earthly Jesus, but he only seemed to be a man. He was not real. He was a spirit who had the appearance of an earthly man. Other Gnostics saw him as totally spirit.

The problem was that as the first century drew to a close the idea of a spiritual Christ did not fit well with the priests and bishops who were developing the foundations of the Catholic Church and their own positions in it.

Around the year 100 CE, Ignatius, the powerful Bishop of Antioch, realized that the religion would be strengthened if the masses could be shown a life story that they could relate to. By now, many years after Paul and the Apostles had had their visions, the people of the diaspora had no idea whether there had ever been a living Jesus or not. It was simply too long ago for them to question anything that they were told.

Ignatius could see that the Gnostic Christians could cause a big problem if the situation could stand as it was. He was not at all happy with the docetic idea that Jesus only seemed to be human, and anyway, the Gnostics had no time for bishops and priests.

The people wanted more information about the godman that was ever more evident in and around the towns of the diaspora.

It was probably Ignatius who decided to create that life story to fill the gap that was causing him some problems. I say probably, but we will never know for sure.

Those gospel writers used information from all over the Empire to create a life story that the people would know and understand, and of course, I relate back to what we said about the Greek, Egyptian and Persian myths, which were so similar, but never identical, to the eventual Jesus creation.

Analysis of the gospels has shown just how brilliantly clever they really are. It is not just the compilation of detail from the mystical east, from the stories of the Buddha and from Krishna, that we find firm foundations, but the stories of the great gods of Greece, Egypt and Persia play a major role too. The stories were contrived to relate to what people knew and probably expected and even more, they were written on different levels.

An outer simple meaning for the non-too profound, with a far deeper allegorical meaning for the more cerebral, with symbolism couched in numbers, understood by only the learned Gnostics and, incredibly, the life of the man was made to mirror the life of the greatest God of all time: the Sun.

And so, at some time at the very end of the first century and into the early second century, Ignatius was probably responsible for the creation of the first of the gospels with the others following as the decades passed.

Deep scholarly investigation has revealed some truly startling elements hidden in the verses of the Bible generally, not just in the New Testament but the Old as well and so very much of it relates to the Sun and its journey through the constellations; something that was hugely important to the ancients.

Chapter 12

Sun of God

Without doubt, the oldest God to be revered by mankind is the star at the centre of our solar system, the Sun. When ancient man gazed in awe and wonderment at the flaming ball in the heavens, he soon understood how vital that source of light and heat was to his own existence.

Peering from their caves, thousands of years ago, our prehistoric ancestors soon realized that the life of the animals and the fruits of the trees and the life of mother earth itself, depended on this celestial body. We can even see evidence of this in the cave paintings of many thousands of years ago, where the Sun seems to play a prominent role in the depictions of their life, preserved for history in their works of primitive art.

History shows that all over the world ancient civilizations were using the Sun as the foundation of their early religious practices and as the centuries passed, the Sun was personified and given an identity that represented the "living" god.

It is universally agreed that the ancient peoples of the world had a deep working knowledge of the stars and celestial bodies above them and, again, history has demonstrated some very interesting finds which relate to star maps composed by our ancient ancestors.

If they knew nothing else, they certainly knew their way around the skies and would use that knowledge to predict the coming of the seasons, vital not only to the hunter gatherers but to the farmers whose crops and animals depended on this seasonal change.

As time progressed the Sun and the stars and their constellations, took on a life of their own. They were turned into manifestations of gods and, as such, demonstrated their own personalities and characteristics. They would represent what we could expect at the time of that particular constellation, such as Aquarius, represented as the Water Bearer that would become associated with the life-giving waters of early spring.

As we continue through this section, you will see, as I did, some truly remarkable elements of Bible history played out, not on earth but in the celestial heavens above us.

It is inconceivable, as you will see, that the passage of the Sun through the constellations did not have a huge influence on the symbolism created in the gospels. Symbolism created by those brilliantly clever Greek storytellers who were very aware of the huge importance that the worship of the Sun and heavens had on just about every religion of the day, including the foundations of all those that preceded them by thousands of years. Christianity was no exception.

This is a developing science, and many scholars are now fully convinced that Christianity is partially based on the concepts of what is now termed astrotheology.

Again, you will find that defenders of the faith, with no comprehension at all of the ancient way of thinking or any knowledge of the history left behind for us to examine, will deny any possibility that astronomy or astrology, the same thing in ancient times, could be possible for the creation of the living Jesus.

As I have asserted several times, without any knowledge of the history of ancient Egypt, Greece, Persia and their gods and myths, you can never understand the origins of the New Testament.

I regularly meet and debate with Christian apologists who have never even heard of the Gnostic gospels. If they display an ignorance of what is most basic in the argument, what chance do I have of explaining the symbolism of the ancient myths and most of all, the foundations of astrotheology. The discussion is pointless: to them it seems, I am an alien.

When we talk about the skies relating to our time in first-century Palestine and the diaspora, I should point out that they did not look exactly as they do today.

A brief astronomy lesson is essential at this point because the whole concept of religion from the stars is based on it.

In the present day, on the morning of the Vernal Equinox, now 21 March, the Sun rises against the background of the constellation of Pisces. If you were able to stand and perceive this annual happening for a very, very long time, then you would be able to see the Sun move across the constellation, and eventually that background constellation would become the constellation of Aquarius.

This progress from one constellation backwards into the next, is as a result of a "wobble" in the earth's axis as it rotates and it's a rotation cycle that takes about 26,000 years to complete.

Because the skies appear differently over this duration, we have what is called the Precession of the Equinoxes.

The twelve constellations of the Zodiac have not really moved, they only appear to be in a different position because of the earth's changing position, due to the "wobble".

As the Sun moves into any one of these signs of the Zodiac, that sign in the background determines the name of the astrological age we live in.

Currently, we are living at the time when at the Vernal Equinox in March, the Sun rises with the background constellation of Pisces: therefore, we are living in the Age of Pisces and will do so for the next 100 years approximately, when the Sun will enter Aquarius. We will then be living in the Age of Aquarius.

This really is the dawning of the Age of Aquarius.

So, for approximately 2160 years we live in the Age of the constellation of the time. As there are twelve signs of the Zodiac, it is a fact that there are 30 degrees of the complete circle in each constellation (twelve x 30 degrees = 360 degrees = the full circle). Therefore, it takes 2160 years to pass through one constellation, but it takes twelve times that to complete the full Zodiac of twelve constellations and that means a total of about 26,000 years before it all starts again. This complete cycle is known as a Great Year or the Platonic Year.

Incredibly, the ancients were fully aware of these movements in the heavens and based their complicated belief systems on those very movements. It was an ancient Greek astronomer called Hipparchus who is reputed to have come up with the observation of the precession of the equinoxes between 162 and 127 BCE. His work changed the face of ancient astrology and astronomy.

Modern scholars believe that the understanding of the concept of the precession goes back very much further than the time of Hipparchus. There are suggestions with good foundation, that the ancient Persians and Egyptians were aware of it as far back as the Age of Taurus, approximately 4700–2500 BCE, depending on the methods of calculation used.

As we said earlier, each of the constellations for the ancients had a personality of their own and each different Age would be expected by them to change the whole nature of existence and that could mean the arrival, too, of an avatar or saving deity for the coming new times.

That the ancient peoples attached solar principles to their gods is self-evident in the historical detail we have available. Virtually all of the gods we have already mentioned in the philosophies and myths of the ancient cultures, have a god who is amongst his many manifestations a Sun god.

We have read in these pages about the worship of the gods Osiris, Horus, Dionysus, Adonis, Mithras and several others, all of whom are solar divinities, revered as Sun gods.

If we take a closer look at the myth of the Sun god Mithras, you will remember the remarkable similarities we discussed in relation to the life of Jesus.

The worship of Mithras was common at the time of the

developing Christian story and shrines and temples have been discovered throughout Europe and even in Scotland.

The temple, or the Mithraeum, an underground cavern, was the scene of the birth of the Saviour, just as Jesus was born in the stable. The chamber is often aligned in a definite position so that on a particular day of celebration, the Sun would pierce the chamber and illuminate the figure of the god within, who would often be depicted with the halo or Sun rays around his head, as Jesus often is.

The focus of the Mithraic temple was the area called the tauroctony, where the sacred bull is pictured being slayed by the Sun god Mithras.

One of the greatest scholars of Mithraism, David Ulansey, in his book *The Origins of the Mithraic Mysteries: Cosmology and Salvation in the Ancient World*, Oxford University Press, 1989, explores the symbolism of what we see in the tauroctony.

Here we see the image of Mithras astride the bull, driving a knife into the neck of the beast. Images of the Sun and moon are often found in association with the signs of the Zodiac and sometimes, too, the scene is flanked on either side by the torch bearers Cautes and Cautopates.

Amongst all of this are images of a dog, snake, raven and scorpion. Everything in the scene can be translated as a cosmic event, with the dog and scorpion etc., being representations of constellations, the whole thing, telling the story of the dawn of Aries.

When the ancient people of the time were made aware of the precession of the equinoxes, they saw their saviour, the Sun god Mithras, as having supernatural powers and for him to alter the very state of the heavens, was proof enough.

Therefore, the image in the tauroctony shows the godman Mithras slaying the bull, which is the bull of the Age of Taurus. all around him are the star constellations which played a major part in their developing myth. The scorpion represents Scorpio, the dog relates to Canis Minor, the snake is Hydra. The two torch bearers, one with his torch facing upwards and the other with his torch facing downwards, represent the two equinoxes of spring and autumn, hugely important events in the life of the Sun as it passes along its ecliptic in the heavens (*Jesus Christ, Sun of God: Ancient Cosmology and Early Christian Symbolism*, David Fideler, Quest Books, 1993).

In his work, David Ulansey concludes by saying,

"Mithraic iconography was a cosmological code created by a circle of religious minded philosophers and scientists to symbolize their possession of secret knowledge: namely, the knowledge of a newly discovered god, so powerful that the entire cosmos was completely under his control."

When the Old Testament writers were creating the myths of Moses at the time of early Hebrew history, it is no coincidence that we should find the great leader getting angry with the people worshipping the Golden Calf.

The writers were making it clear that Moses was the avatar of the new Age and the calf was a throwback representation to the old Age of Taurus and everything that went with it.

Now, the new Age of Aries would see the almighty Sun in a new House of the Zodiac and from now on, religious imagery would involve the lamb and the ram, symbolic of the new cosmic month. Throughout this time we have gods depicted with the horns of the ram, like Zeus Ammon for instance.

Progressing through the Age, we ultimately see the end of the Age of Aries marked by the death of Jesus, the slaying of "the sacrificial lamb of God" and also depicted as the avatar of the new Age, in the form of the Messiah heralding the Age of Pisces and all that fishy iconography that we see associated with Christianity.

It was Thomas Paine (1737–1809), one of America's founding fathers who said, "The Christian religion is a parody on the worship of the Sun, in which they put a man whom they call

Christ in the place of the Sun and pay him the same adoration which was originally paid to the Sun" (*The Theological Works of Thomas Paine*, Wentworth Press, 2019).

Jesus, like so many of the solar gods, shares similar attributes with those that came before him.

Let us look at one remarkable feature, essential to the truth behind the revelation of the supposedly unique to the Christian religion, but common to many earlier myths.

We have discussed at some length the fact that so many Sun gods are supposedly "born" on 25 December, or near to it. It did not take the Catholic Church long to adopt this date, as well, as the birth date of their Saviour.

To relate this to the life of the Sun we must understand that the Sun moves through a cycle of its own life and death as the seasons come and go.

At the end of December it was noticed by all those ancient peoples that the Sun was getting ever weaker, and their deity appeared to be dying. On 21 December, the Sun has reached its lowest point in the sky and appears not to move any higher in the sky. This is the Winter Solstice.

For three days their Saviour, the Sun, appears to be dead, lying somewhere in a tomb on the other side of the horizon.

On the night of 24 December, the faithful would await the Sunrise the following morning, when miraculously, they could celebrate the birth of their god as it began to climb higher in the sky again and they could look forward to another cycle of the rebirth of light. Their Saviour was born on 25 December.

Their celebrations continued at the time of the Vernal Equinox, the time we call Easter, when the hours of light become longer than the hours of darkness. Their god had truly resurrected and would live again for another cycle of celestial adventures.

This was used constructively by the Christian gospel writers. They were well aware of the Sun's cosmic life cycle and that all the followers of Mithras, Osiris, Horus and many more, had already absorbed the cosmic significance of the Sun's cycle. They made their Jesus fit in as yet another Sun god, something the people would understand and revere.

Jesus lived out the heavenly cycle perfectly. The birth of the baby Jesus on 25 December reflects the birth of the newly born Sun. At the time of midnight on the 24th, the constellation of Virgo, the virgin, is rising on the horizon. This is the Virgin birth of the Saviour, that is, the birth of the new Sun in conjunction with the constellation of the virgin.

At the time of this "virgin birth", at the lower end of the star formation known as Orion's Belt, there are three significant stars known as the "Three Kings". If a line is drawn through these stars they point in the direction of the brightest star in the sky, Sirius. You can see where this is going can't you?

So here we have a "heavenly" story where at midnight on 24 December we have three "Kings" apparently following a sign, a star in the sky, which indicates the point on the horizon where the Sunrise, the God, will be "born" in conjunction with "the virgin", rising above that horizon.

This is self-evidently the story of a virgin birth and it gets even more remarkable.

The Sun on its apparent passage through the heavens moves along an imaginary circle in the sky, which connects all the signs of the Zodiac. This plane or circular path is called the Ecliptic and the Sun, as it grows stronger from its birth in December, moves along it, passing through each of the signs of the Zodiac as it does so.

Now, if you can imagine the earth's equator, that imaginary ring around the centre of the earth, expanded out into space, then that, too, will create another imaginary circle around Mother Earth.

Because both circles are drawn at different angles, they will at two points in space intersect and cross each other.

At the time of the Vernal Equinox in March, our Easter,

the Sun is situated firmly on the point where the two circles intersect and cross each other. As we said earlier, the Vernal Equinox marks the true resurrection of the Sun as it defeats the powers of darkness and the days are longer than the nights.

This can be expressed as the "resurrection" of the God, the Sun Jesus, from the "cross", the intersection of the celestial circles at the time of Easter.

In a nutshell, the Sun Jesus, born of a virgin, constellation of Virgo, on 25 December. Sun's rebirth at Solstice, marked by a significant star, Sirius, followed by three kings, King stars of Orion's Belt, with the resurrection from the cross at Easter, the equinox and of course, that day which we celebrate, is always a Sunday, the day of the Lord – a Sun Day.

The significance of the constellation of Virgo should not be underestimated.

The figure depicted by the stars in the sign of the Zodiac is depicted as holding an ear of wheat in her left hand, the star Spica. As you know, the signs or constellations of the Zodiac are referred to as Houses. The connotations of wheat in the constellation of Virgo indicate this as the "House of Bread" and in Hebrew, the name Bethlehem, means the "house of bread". The godman, born in Bethlehem, the "house of bread". Born not on earth but in the constellations above.

There are plenty of doubters who point out that the Bible never mentions the birth date of Jesus and how could shepherds be watching their flocks of sheep in the fields at such an unlikely time in mid-winter?

That is very true if we are talking about an earthly happening and an earthly birth but if we are involved in a celestial allegory, then it is very possible.

The reason is, if we are involved here in the birth of the Sun, the shepherds and the sheep we read about are actually stars as well.

Within the constellation of Cepheus there are two stars called

Errai and Alfirk.

Amazingly, these names mean shepherd and flock, respectively. So, in the celestial story at the time, nearby to the miraculous birth of the saviour Sun Jesus, there really were shepherds and flocks doing what shepherds and flocks do.

So here we have the exact story as we all know it, reflected perfectly in the heavenly world above us. Again, the Sun was personified as a being, whether it was Horus, Osiris, Dionysus, Mithras, or Jesus the Christ; they were all given the Sun's life story as it passed through the constellations.

Where do you think the twelve disciples came from? As the Sun travelled through its celestial journey it moved in conjunction with its twelve disciples, the signs of the Zodiac! This number twelve has a huge significance to the writers of the Old and New Testaments and is deeply rooted in ancient numerology and gematria.

Its significance is obvious from the times we see it used. We read of the twelve Tribes of Israel, Jacob had twelve sons and the personality of each of them was used to describe each Sun sign we know today. We read of twelve great Patriarchs, twelve gates and twelve angels in the Book of Revelation, and that is before we consider twelve months in a year, twelve days of Christmas and so on.

The twelve Disciples are symbolic of the twelve tribes of Israel, and the twelve Tribes are themselves symbolic of the signs of the ancient Zodiac.

Just as Jesus is depicted as being surrounded by twelve disciples, so, too, is the Sun god Mithras.

"The Mithraic disciples were dressed up to represent the twelve signs of the zodiac and circled the initiate, who represented Mithras himself" (Timothy Freke and Peter Gandy, *The Jesus Mysteries: Was The 'Original Jesus' A Pagan God?* Thorsons, 1999).

The solar symbolism is everywhere. As the Sun apparently

moves through the constellations it works its way through the thirty degrees of each zodiacal sign in the cycle and, of course, Jesus was thirty years old when he began his ministry.

The historian Acharya S, in her impressively researched work *Origins of Christianity* points out:

The Sun (Jesus) is the "Light of the World."

The Sun (Jesus) "cometh on clouds and every eye shall see him."

The Sun (Jesus) rising in the morning is the "saviour of mankind."

The Sun (Jesus) wears a corona, crown of thorns or a halo.

The Sun (Jesus) walks on water. The reflection of the solar orb as it hangs above a stretch of water.

The biblical references to the solar deity and the links with the book's great characters are abundant. My own local church has a board outside reading, "Jesus. The Light of the World."

In John 8:12, we read the well-known declaration, "I am the light of the world; anyone who follows me will not be walking in the dark but will have the light of life."

It appears regularly in the Old Testament and as Ezekiel lamented when he had to admit that Sun worship was popular, "and he brought me into the inner court of the Lord's house and behold, at the door of the Temple of the Lord, between the porch and the altar, were about five and twenty men, with their backs toward the Temple of the Lord and their faces towards the east; and they worshipped the Sun towards the east" (Ezekiel 8:16).

And why did the sky darken at the time of the supposed death of Jesus on the cross, as related by the gospel writers? Well, if Jesus is the earthly manifestation of the Sun god, then his death really would result in darkness for all mankind. The Sun was dead.

Much of the solar symbolism in both the Old and New Testaments is not always easy to identify without some considerable knowledge of the Sun and star movements in the skies above. This was some knowledge which our ancient ancestors certainly did possess.

References to Light of the World and many others with a direct relationship to "light" are easy to understand as solar allegories, some of the best-known stories in the gospels are immersed in solar and stellar symbolism but have gone unnoticed to the astronomically unaware since they were created.

Isaiah tells us quite clearly that the God of the Bible is a manifestation of the eternal Sun god. In Isaiah 60:19 he says: "The Sun will no more be your light by day, nor will the brightness of the moon shine on you, for the Lord will be your everlasting light and your god will be your glory."

The Book of Malachi makes the point as well, "But for you who revere my name, the Sun of righteousness will rise with healings in its wings. And you will go out and leap like calves released from the stall" (Malachi 4:2).

There is a reference in Isaiah 27:1, which reads, "In that day Jehovah with his hard and great and strong sword, will punish Leviathan the swift serpent and Leviathan the crooked serpent; and he will slay the monster that is in the sea."

This is a symbolic reference to the eternal battle between light and dark. Just as Horus the young Sun god of the Egyptians fought the cosmic battle with the evil Set so that light would ultimately rule the world, then this early story from the Hebrew Bible tells of something similar.

The constellation of Hydra, the sea serpent, which is one of the largest constellations, was defeating the power of the Sun as the night fell and Hydra ruled the sky.

With the coming daylight, Jehovah would again defeat the evil serpent and so the battle would continue.

The snake serpent motif has represented darkness and evil in many cultures over the millennia and can also be perceived in some myths as a symbol of wisdom.

Greek mythology tells the story of the great Sun god Apollo

killing the serpent Python in the hills near Delphi and there is also that great bedtime story of the Sun god Heracles who fought the seven-headed Hydra, taking some considerable time to get round the seven heads problem.

Even the story of Judas can be translated in an astrotheological way. As the Sun passes through the thirty degrees of the constellation of Sagittarius, the god gets ever weaker and meets his doom at the very start of Capricorn. The thirty degrees is the thirty pieces of silver paid before his eventual death. As we will see in the chapter relating to the ancient art/science of gematria, every number mentioned in the Bible has a far deeper significance than what at first appears.

That number thirty keeps popping up. We mentioned that Jesus began his works at the age of thirty. This comes from the fact that the birth of the Sun at the Solstice at the time of the creation of the Jesus Sun (Son) myth would have been under the constellation of Capricorn; this would have represented the power of darkness and the influence of Saturn. It takes thirty degrees of movement for the Sun to escape the clutches of this threatening sign of the Zodiac. He then begins his ministry at the age of thirty.

Incredibly, the story goes on in a solar and stellar sense to explain the truth behind the myth of Herod and the massacre of the innocents; a story, you will remember, that exists in other religious cults which we have discussed before and that have their roots firmly planted in the heavens, as well. The story of the Sun and its life as it passed through the heavens was a universal myth understood by ancient communities all over the world. The ancients watched the Sun and the Moon, and the stars and turned them into figures of worship: something the Christians did just as competently as everybody else.

The story of Herod does not of course have any references in the works of the historians of the day. Not a word from Josephus or Philo, both of whom could not have ignored such a heinous crime. They did not ignore it: they simply did not know about it. It did not happen on earth; it all took place in the skies above.

It is often quoted by scholars who study the astrotheological origins of Christianity, that the one-year story of Jesus Christ and his works is an allegorical representation of the Sun as it moves through the signs. Even the events depicted in the gospel stories can be related to the characteristics of each of the signs.

Jesus even speaks in the language of the stars, something that would have been understood by those who were spiritually aware.

When the disciples ask Jesus about the end of the world and how long Jesus will be with them, Matt 24:3 and Matt 28:20 tells them he will be with them until the end of the world. This is a mistranslation from the original Greek and should read until the end of the "Age", which, you will understand from our previous discussions, means the end of the "Age of Pisces", when a new Age will dawn and possibly a new messianic figure will emerge.

Similarly, when the twelve ask the boss where the next Passover will be (Luke 22:10), Jesus replies by saying, "Behold, when you are entered into the city, there shall a man meet you bearing a pitcher of water. Follow him into the house where he enters in."

This is obviously more of the same. Jesus is telling them that the man with the pitcher of water is the figure, the water bearer, which depicts the sign of Aquarius. When he says enter his house, he means enter the sign and this will herald the new Age of Aquarius. The Sun will have moved on into its new Age.

Jesus was made to say and play out the significance of the Ages he related to. The sacrificial lamb of God was Jesus at the end of the Age of Aries and at the start of the Age of Pisces, everything takes on a distinctly fishy motif.

The first thing he does at the start of his magnificent works is to go out and round up a bunch of fishermen as disciples and then calls them "fishers of men".

Jesus feeds five thousand people with nothing more than a couple of fishes and some bread, a story, which will amaze you when we look at the real significance in the next chapter.

Even the word "fish" in Greek, which is "Ichthus", was taken by early Christians and using each individual letter, composed "Iesous Christus Theou Uios soter", which translates as "Jesus Christ, Son of God, Saviour".

The Sun and stars are truly everywhere in the Bible stories. They go totally unnoticed unless you know what you are looking for and as a result, most of the Christian faithful have no idea how much solar, stellar and, indeed, lunar symbolism is written in the pages of the Old and New Testaments.

The clues are not always easy to spot but those with "eyes to see and ears to hear", would know immediately the solar significances of what was being told.

The story of John the Baptist, his conception, birth, beheading and the baptism of Jesus is yet another myth constructed in the heavens.

We can, from the stories told by the gospel writers, work out the time and age differences between Jesus and John the Baptist, dates which are verified by the scholarly Catholic Encyclopaedia.

The birth of John is calculated and celebrated when Aquarius is at its zenith, at the time of the Summer Solstice, 24 June. Aquarius is the sign of the water bearer and, of course, John is the baptizer: an obvious water connection.

The gospels tell us too, that John baptizes Jesus when the Sun is in the house of Aquarius, that is, the God baptized by the water bearer.

John's birth, supposedly at the time of the Summer Solstice is a firm indication that Jesus' birth was at the time of the Winter Solstice, because the gospels indicate a six-month gap in their ages. John marks Jesus as a solar deity when he declares, "He must increase, but I must decrease" (John 3:26).

This is clearly a reference to the solar concept of the Sun getting weaker after the Summer Solstice but getting stronger from its birth on 25 December.

The Gospel of Luke tells us about the angel coming to Mary six months after the divine conception of Elizabeth, the mother of John. So, with the stories before us and some detective work on the dates, we can relate the stories of Jesus' baptism and birth with the works of John the Baptist, in a purely astronomical sense. Even the beheading of the Baptizer is explained allegorically in the starry night sky.

Interesting too, I think you'll agree, that in the birth of John the Baptist, we have yet another example of a miraculous conception and one that goes largely unnoticed.

Elizabeth, who was barren and of advanced years (see Luke 1:5), was suddenly pregnant after divine intervention. "But the angel said to him, 'Do not be afraid Zechariah, for your prayer is heard and your wife Elizabeth will bear you a son and you shall call his name John'" (Luke 1:13).

As we keep seeing, as we go through our quest, there were miraculous births everywhere, including the miraculous conception of Samson to a barren woman, announced by the obligatory angel naturally, who then matures into the Old Testament superhero with solar attributes. His name in the original Hebrew is Shimshon, the root of which means "Sun" (*The Gospel and the Zodiac: The Secret Truth About Jesus*, Bill Darlison, Gerald Duckworth & Co Ltd, 2009).

Samson, as the Sun deity, rues the day he took up with Delilah, whose name relates to "water bucket", the name in Hebrew for the constellation of Aquarius. In his remarkable work, Rev. Bill Darlison explains that when the Sun was in Aquarius, the god (Samson) was still very weak and when Delilah cut his flowing locks, that is, cut away his life-giving rays, the Sun was doomed.

Darlinson's research demonstrates clearly just how so much of the Gospel of Mark relates in some way to the life of the Sun

Jesus as it passes along the ecliptic and visits each of the signs of the Zodiac, each with their own personalities and symbolism.

He points out, just as we discussed earlier, that gospel stories are written on different levels and are not meant to be read as literal, historical events. His implication is that the gospels have been misread for nearly two thousand years and I am inclined to agree with him and surprisingly, he is a minister in the Unitarian Church.

Clearly, in those very early times, ancient man had a profound fear of darkness and all things associated with it.

If the life of crops and animals depended on the life-giving properties of the Sun, then the powers of darkness would have to be defeated, so it was not surprising that they gave the Sun gods as much support as they could in that important task.

Christianity was just another of the long line of cults that adopted the figure of a saviour and imbued him with the aspects of the Sun and its solar life cycle.

The early orthodox Christians were aligning the birth and resurrection of their Son of God with the Sun at the time of the Solstice and the Equinox, and the similarities are hard to ignore!

It is no coincidence that all those mystery religions we described earlier, were equally aware of the solar story and that is why their godmen were so very similar to Jesus.

The early concept of vegetative gods and the living and dying cycle of the crops, eventually fused with the Sun's life story and then saviours were created to maintain the eternal cycle of life and death. They all shared the same basic motifs.

We spent some time examining the lives of the godmen of the Greek and Egyptian civilizations and you will remember how they all demonstrate a miraculous birth and often a virgin birth. They all share the Winter Solstice as a birth date, and usually, are born in a cave or stable or underground chamber, at that time. Even the stable of Jesus comes from the Augean stables of the Sun god Hercules, which has a close association with the zodiacal sign of Capricorn.

Each of the heroes toiled tirelessly for the good of mankind and faced all sorts of trials and tribulations as they did so. This is demonstrated by the Sun Jesus fighting off the powers of darkness in his early life, like the story in the stars about Herod searching for the newborn Sun Jesus and carrying out the "massacre of the innocents". Again, this celestial tale is known and told by other religious cultures. Capricorn as a power of darkness is the great threat to the newborn Sun who struggles to avoid his clutches.

The life story continues, and the ultimate "resurrection" is celebrated at the time of the equinox. As with Jesus, so it was with Adonis and Tammuz, it was this Vernal Equinox that had, as we said earlier, massive significance for the priests of the many cults that followed it.

We have seen how the zodiac behind the rising Sun on the morning of the equinox gives the name to the age we live in. This had a huge significance on the "characteristics" of the Sun god saviour associated with it.

We have seen how Mithras, the Sun god who competed with Jesus for adoration at the time, was depicted as slaying the bull as a representation of the end of the Age of Taurus and heralding the new Age of Aries the lamb or ram.

Then, so too did Jesus play his part as the Sun god when, at the end of the Age of Aries, when the Sun Jesus finally passed over the equinox and into a new Age of Pisces, he as the Sun would symbolically "slay the lamb of God" and be slain himself as the man as it passed over.

This sacrifice was the promise of redemption, and probably the reason we see early depictions of Jesus with a lamb around his shoulders.

The Mithraic followers, too, shared a reverence for the slayed bull and rejoiced in the washing in the blood of the slain bull, just as the Christians would go on to use the expression, "washed in the blood of the lamb".

You will remember, however, that the Mithraic cult really did bathe in the blood of the slaughtered animal and perceived this to wash away their sins and a way to eternal life.

As an interesting aside, in ancient art, the first representation we have of Jesus is as a man with the lamb around him. Incredibly, it is not until the seventh century CE that we see the first examples of Christian art depicting the man on a cross, and of those, the earlier works show a man on a stake.

Strangely enough, as the centuries have passed, you would think that the Church would have tried to rid itself of any of those solar symbols that had such a close link with paganism and the true roots of their Christian belief.

Well, they never did. Solar symbolism is still so very evident in churches and cathedrals around the world that you can only assume that the true significance is not understood by the masses.

The Wheel of the Zodiac is a symbol, which is pagan in origin and relates to the passage of the Sun through the Equinoxes and the Solstices and over the millennia, has appeared in different forms.

In a simple version, it is shown as a circle with a cross dividing it into four equal quadrants. Those four quadrants are broken down into three equal slices, giving a total of twelve equal divisions. These divisions represent the signs of the zodiac and the four quarters represent the four seasons.

The cross which divides the whole circle is the representation of the two Solstices and the two Equinoxes: the line of the equinoxes at right angles to the line of the solstices.

This is how the ancient stargazers and myth writers perceived the movement of their solar hero in relation to the zodiacal signs. As the Sun moved on the lines of the cross, it was easy to see how they could translate the death of the god in terms of "dying on the cross" and at the Vernal Equinox, "resurrecting from the cross".

This symbol, the original pagan wheel of the zodiac depicting the Sun's movements and its life and death, is still used on church steeples to this day.

If you extend the cross within the circle so that it protrudes out of the circle, you have the very familiar cross with a ring around it, seen on thousands of churches around the world!

Similarly, if you take the cross in its accepted form in Christianity today, that cross was used to symbolize the characteristics of the equinoxes and solstices, in as much as the long portion of the perpendicular beam of the cross depicted the longer days of the Summer Solstice, while the shorter portion depicted the shorter, darker days.

The equal proportions of the cross beam were the depiction of the equality of the equinoxes between spring and autumn.

Going into churches reveals a whole series of solar representations, which hark back to the very beginning of the Christian story and its solar origins.

For years I never really knew what the letters IHS stand for, which are commonly seen on wall hangings and on various bits of church furniture, in fact, all over churches!

If you ask three church people what the origin and significance of this letter grouping is, you will probably get four answers.

Not many people know the true origin and several suggestions have been put forward and all seem quite acceptable.

The commonest explanation is that it comes from the first three letters of the name of Jesus in Greek and was a shortened form of his sacred name.

Another possibility put forward is that it stands for Iesus Hominum Salvator, or Jesus, Saviour of Men.

Another is what Constantine is reputedly responsible for when he saw a sacred sign in the sky with the inscription, "In Hoc Signo Vinces", meaning, "In this sign, you shall conquer" (Eusebius, *The Life of Constantine*).

Various investigators, including the historian Acharya S in her work *The Origins of Christianity*, have pointed out that the IHS symbol is related to the mystical name of Bacchus, the Sun god.

Of course, Bacchus, in his other manifestation, is the godman we discussed at length, known as Dionysus.

Not only was our friend Bacchus associated with the godman Dionysus but he was also regarded in ancient culture as the young returning Sun deity known as Tammuz, who is mentioned in the Old Testament as the Sun god, much lamented by the weeping women at the Jewish Temple.

It gets even worse for those who deny the solar deity in the churches. The letters IHS are also sometimes seen on the stained-glass windows, surrounded by the golden rays of the Sun! I think the early fathers really did know where it all came from.

IHS often appears on the monstrance too. The monstrance is the ornate vessel used in the church to display the consecrated Eucharistic host and not only does it often display the IHS symbol of Bacchus, but the vessel itself is often one huge Sunburst, with the host at its centre. The host itself sometimes carries the solar symbol.

Before we leave the subject of solar worship as the root of Christian myth making, I think it would be interesting to mention that the Cathedral of Notre Dame de Liesse at Annecy in France and nearby churches, are aligned to the Summer Solstice Sun and inside, the works of art show definite links to the Sun and its path in the heavens.

A painting of Jesus, *I am the light of the world*, shows four signs of the zodiac in each of the corners of the artwork. The four signs, Aquarius, Scorpio, Leo and Taurus, if depicted on the Wheel of the Zodiac, form a cross. Christ's aura, or halo of light always depicted around his head, is a throwback to the halo of Helios, the great Sun god and is often shown, in the case of Jesus, with a cross planted within it.

The stained-glass window which carries the image of Mary and Child, is also framed by the four zodiacal signs, and I wonder why the statue of the Black Madonna and Child has her head surrounded by twelve stars representing the Zodiac?

The fingers, arms, and hands of the characters depicted all demonstrate angles of 23.5 degrees. This is of huge significance because that is the angle of the earth's axis relative to that of the ecliptic and that opens a whole can of worms about the precession of equinoxes.

Sun worship is as old as mankind himself and that it should develop over thousands of years into a religion personified by a mythical being representing the power of that Sun, is no surprise.

The Sun was the centre of the great religions of Egypt, Persia and Greece and let's not forget, was also an important part of the early worship of the Hebrew people.

To claim that it had no influence on the myriad of cultic beliefs that ultimately created the fledgling faith of Christianity, I think, simply has no foundation. We have already seen how that early Jewish sect of the Essenes and the Therapeutae, recorded by Philo and their Church of God associated with Paul, were Sun worshippers.

It was probably these Gnostic thinking Essenes and their close relatives the Therapeutae, who eventually gave rise to the Christian movement. Their influence would be deeply rooted in the fledgling faith and they brought their Sun worship with them.

The later gospel writers, brilliant scholars of the time and immersed in the mythology of the many solar gods surrounding them, would then go on to use much of the myth from competing beliefs and use the well-known elements of the solar deities to create a life, death and resurrection story for their man, giving him a life story, that never really existed. The life, death and rebirth cycle of the vegetative god motif and that of the dying and resurrecting Sun were brought together.

The gospels tell fantastic stories which offer great spiritual insight but were certainly never meant to be believed as history. The stories relate to events which mirror the seasons and the trials and tribulations of the Sun of God as it fought its way through the solar year. Conveniently, for the early Church fathers, those stories became real history and have influenced the development of the western world for two thousand years. The early bishops knew very well that it was in their best interest to let it take its course and give them the authority they craved.

In our discussion about the solar god influence on Christianity, we have but only scratched the surface! The subject, like our previous investigations in earlier chapters, requires a book of its own.

The work of David Fideler is a piece of pure scholarship. He never tries to be sensationalist in any way and tells the story of early Hellenistic religions through to Christianity via solar worship and the highly complicated science of gematria.

It is that subject of gematria that we will now consider, and if you thought that Sun god issues caused a few questions to be asked in your mind, you will not believe what this much overlooked element of ancient philosophy will bring up!

Chapter 13

The Divine Equation

When I started my research into the origins of the Christian movement, many years ago, I was stunned to uncover the facts that had been known to some scholars, for probably centuries. The similarities between the ancient gods and the Christian Jesus amazed me, especially when I learnt more about the miraculous births, the resurrections and even the famous sayings that were so very similar.

It made me realize that there was a lot more to the well-known story than I was ever led to believe.

I was off on an epic journey that has taken me through more than twenty years of wonder and absolute amazement and included, for several of those years, an in-depth study of the history of pagan beliefs.

This proved to be an incredibly interesting study and I was surprised to find so much early Christian philosophy involved in traditional pagan traditions.

They too, like all the early mystery religions, tell of a godman, a god of the forest, who gives up his life at the end of an agricultural season, descends into the underworld and comes back again to start another agricultural cycle.

His goddess, the goddess of the Moon, plays her part in the annual cycle and between them, they defeat the powers of darkness and bring about all things good for their followers. The seasons, the stars and the moon play a major part in their ceremony. In effect, they are nature worshippers and most certainly do not worship the Devil of the Bible.

These are obviously the white witches that we often read about and on the face of it, seem to be a harmless bunch who genuinely seem to want to revere the spirit of nature. It may surprise you to know that they believe in an all-powerful cosmic creator, who is represented by the various names of the Moon Goddess: she of many names.

The point I am making is that all these religious philosophies from the very early Zoroastrian and Egyptian beliefs of 3500 years ago and more, to the founding of the Christian Church 2000 years ago, all shared the same basic motifs in one form or another, and that stunned me because I thought Christianity was a one-off, unique revelation and there was nothing else like it.

As surprised as I was, nothing prepared me for what unfolded when I learnt about the system of Gematria and Sacred Geometry, employed by ancient philosophers to conceal more profound, deeper spiritual significance to stories which could thus be read on various levels of understanding. A story could be written and understood as a spiritual message, even by children, but deep within, concealed in the numbers of the gematria, was a second, more meaningful message, meant for those who were taught in the mystery of the science.

The Greek and Hebrew alphabets are quite special in that a Greek letter is also a number and conversely, a number is also a letter. The same situation exists in the Hebrew alphabet. Thus, if you write a word or a sentence, those words add up to a number and that number can demonstrate a special significance.

Scholars of gematria always quote the early usage of gematria as recorded on a clay tablet, which tells the story of King Sargon 11 (circa 720 BCE), who built the walls of his city of Khorsabad to the dimensions of his name. The tablet tells us that the walls were 16,283 cubits, which is the arithmetical value of his name. In a very simple sense, he was as one with his city. However, the use of gematria gets a lot more complicated than this.

The Pythagoreans and the Egyptians before them, revered numbers as divine and were associated with the divine powers. The ancients perceived the cosmos as built on numbers and certain numbers played a major role in their civilization and the nature of their gods.

The use of numbers became almost a language and by introducing sacred numbers into their texts and indeed their architecture, they could conceal secret esoteric meanings and convey divine attributes on their temples by including the number of the gods in the dimensions of the structures.

The biblical scholar Margaret Starbird puts it well when she says, "the practice of gematria is like setting lyrics to music; in the Bible and other texts, significant phrases were carefully and deliberately set to numbers" (Margaret Starbird, *Magdalene's Lost Legacy: Symbolic Numbers and the Sacred Union in Christianity*, Bear & Company, 2003).

The temples, sacred sites and pyramids of antiquity were built with sacred numbers enclosed and if, for example, that temple was dedicated to the great god Apollo, then the number 1061, the gematria of the name, would be very obvious in the structural dimensions.

From time immemorial it appears that the ancient civilizations of Egypt and Greece used a Canon of sacred numbers which carried the harmonious proportions that they based their civilizations on.

Some of these numbers were composed to relate to each other, like the names of the Greek gods, while others came from the natural measurements of the earth and moon and incredibly, much of it came out of the ratio of musical intervals.

At the beginning of my work in this subject, I found the whole business of gematria and sacred geometry to be almost incomprehensible! It took a lot of work to understand what it was and why it was used by those ancient Pythagoreans and Christian Gnostics; it is for this very reason that the subject has gone almost unnoticed by almost all of the world of theological academia, and certainly by the doctors of divinity associated with a purely Christian message to defend. They will find gematria and its significance not only incompatible with their subject, but the implications from what comes out of it will stun them.

Before we look at examples of how it was used, we must understand that the subject is not to be looked at like some conspiracy theory based on a strange code in the Bible that predicts the end of the world and maybe, even if my football team will ever win a trophy.

This is something which is well known about by some historians and has been for thousands of years but very few, until more recent times, have bothered delving into this science, which is a lifetime study.

That the Pythagoreans used it in their philosophical writings is self-evident. It is there to be seen. It is not a theory. It is real.

Similarly, the Christian writers of early Gnosticism and indeed the gospel writers themselves, were self-evidently students of the Pythagorean school, for the evidence, once again, is there to be seen. It is not a theory. It is real. The numbers which were used as revealing deeper truths, that is numbers of the *Ancient Canon of Number* and their geometric proportions, are there in the pages of the New and Old Testament, for all to see.

The Pythagoreans, hundreds of years before the advent of Christianity, saw the numbers between one and ten as having individual properties and when displayed as an equilateral triangle made up of ten dots to represent one to ten, this to them was a symbol of the created universe, as was the Tree of Life to their Jewish mystic equivalents. From this triangle, the numbers one to four were at the basis of creation itself, and this triangle of creation was known as the Tetractys.

The numbers were scrutinized for their properties and a philosophy developed around that number. The number seven, for instance, was perceived as a very special number because it cannot be multiplied by any other number to create another number in the first ten of the triangle, and also, it is not the product of any of those numbers either. it was considered the virgin number and because the multiple of 1 to 7 is 28, it took on significance with the female menstrual cycle and the Moon.

Eight was a cube number, that is 2 squared, and as a cube with six sides and eight vertices, was a symbol of stability. If these individual numbers were expressed in a triple form, like 111, 888 or 444, they took on an enhanced meaning.

The element of three had a special place and any number that could be broken down to three, was also looked upon as special. As we have said, the three sides of the equilateral triangle were the building blocks of the whole cosmos.

One of the greatest scholars of ancient times, Plato (429–347 BCE), was the author of one of the best-known pieces of ancient Greek philosophy *The Laws*, which depicts his idea of the idealised city: the City of Magnesia.

This city is described accurately and even tells us how many citizens that it should house. The dimensions of its walls and ground area are perfectly defined and the whole is based on the canon of number.

These numbers, very many of which are multiples of the number 72, which itself is a product of the mystical twelve which appears everywhere in the Bible, were evident in much of his construction. Numbers such as 5040, 3168, 7920, 1440, 1224 and 1080 and so many more, had immense significance in their meanings.

As we have already discussed, many of these numbers were calculated from the natural dimensions of the earth, Sun and Moon and these were used to bring together heaven and earth by creating a heaven on earth.

These numbers have been shown by the respected writer John Michell (1933–2009) in his book *City of Revelation: On the Proportions and Symbolic Numbers of the Cosmic Temple*, Abacus Books, 1973, to have been sacred to far earlier civilizations before the Greeks. His work in this field has revealed again and again, that it's there for all to see, that the numbers demonstrated by Plato, in his City of Magnesia, are the same foundation dimensions as are found in the structure and layout of the Bronze Age Stonehenge and incredibly, in the dimensions of the New Jerusalem as described in St John's Revelation in the New Testament.

This relationship is hugely important in the numbers of the gospels, as we shall see later.

The appearance of sacred numbers in each of these ancient sites is no coincidence. The numbers were included because they had to be. They were the numbers of harmony between heaven and earth, the microcosm within the macrocosm.

Let's have a look at just a few of these significant numbers and see how they relate to each other.

The canon is quite extensive but certain numbers make a regular appearance and obviously have supreme importance. It is more than coincidence that 3168 appears as a principal number in the measurements of Stonehenge, Plato's ideal city and then again in the New Jerusalem of the New Testament.

The number has some very interesting properties and appears naturally in many ways, in fact in some truly remarkable ways.

If you take the distance of the Sun from the earth as 93 million miles, which is the accepted mean distance, then convert the miles to inches and then divide this number by the speed of light, 186,000 mph, you will get the answer of 3168. (The zeros can be ignored; it is the digits that count.)

If you draw a square around the earth, which has a diameter of 7920 miles, the perimeter of that square will equal 4 x 7920, which equals 31,680. (Again, ignore the zeros.)

The diameter of the Sun is 316800 Megalithic miles.

The diameter of the Moon is 2160 miles, a square drawn around this circle will have a perimeter of 3168 megalithic miles. (1 Megalithic mile = 2.7272 miles.)

The dimensions of the Ark given to Noah by God to escape the shower add up to that ever-present number of 3168 cubits.

With the diameter of the earth accepted as 7920 miles and the diameter of the Moon accepted as 2160 miles, if you place these two circles tangential to each other and enclose the whole in one large circle, that will have a circumference of 31680 miles, assuming pi in the geometrical calculation to be 22/7.

There are more of these naturally occurring examples and you can work them out and see for yourself that the figures add up.

At this point, I should bring in an element of the study that will give you something to think about. These numbers appear in the gematria of the Bible stories. The Bible writers were well aware of the significance of ancient numbers, and they used them to conceal meanings within simple stories.

If you write "Lord Jesus Christ" in the original Greek and then work out its arithmetical value in gematria, guess what the number is! Yes, it is 3168.

This was already a number of ancient origin and meaning, even at the time of the writing of the gospel stories. The early Christians knew what they were doing when they invented His name Iesous! (It is the three words "Lord Jesus Christ" which add up to 3168.)

We said that individual numbers between one and ten had their own characteristics. The number 7 was the virgin number and the number of spiritual perfection; number 8 was a number of regeneration and a new beginning and number 4 was considered the number of the earth.

If you multiply the diameter of the earth, 7920, by four, you will get the inevitable 31680.

To relate to a few more examples, let us look at the relationship of the Earth and Moon diameters. If you add that of the Moon, 1080 miles, to that of the earth, 3960 miles, you get 5040. You will remember that this number was significant in the Platonic design and also in the New Testament's New Jerusalem. An extra thing to think about is that the product of all the letters in the Greek word for Christ is 5040.

The number 3168 shows itself in so many natural elements of our universe that it is hard to believe that the Greek writers of biblical times did not know the value when they used it in their designs and His title. We could go on from here and examine its appearance in the dimensions of the pyramids and even a geometrical calculation involving the distance of the planets from the Sun, results in the figure 3168 but this could and would take up many, many pages.

Sacred numbers came from other sources too. It was that genius Pythagoras who studied the mathematics of music. It is only when you read how profound his knowledge was of the harmonic ratios and the mathematical ratios of the perfect fourth and the perfect fifth, using a monochord instrument, can you begin to see his true genius.

There are works of real scholarship that explain the music and mathematical relationships and without a real deep understanding of the structure of music, it is almost impossible to comprehend. Sadly, I do not possess that understanding and can only report the findings of Pythagoras and subsequent investigators as to what we have gained from their work.

The ancient Greeks looked at music as a sacred mystical study and the revealer of the mysteries based on number. The god Apollo was the god of Music and was seen as the manifestation of light. He was also the god that represented the Sun.

The names of the early Greek gods were no accident. They were constructed to harmonize with each other and to reveal mathematical symbolism that was the basis for the design of sacred geometry, which again, would demonstrate the true meaning of a story using the proof of geometry.

The work of Pythagoras demonstrates some wonderful mathematics going on in the heart of musical harmony. Plato recognized this and how the Egyptians were aware of it too, when he pointed out that their civilization had thrived for centuries on the numbers they lived by, based on their harmonics of music.

In a way he was saying that only certain mathematical ratios of music were allowed, so no rock and roll there then.

Pythagoras was able to work out two critical ratios within music and these came from his analysis of the perfect fourth and the perfect fifth. Two numbers from this which we should be aware of are:

In Pythagorean musical proportion, the perfect 5th is expressed as the ratio of 6:9. From this he deduced by simple maths the number 0.666 (6 divided by 9). The number 666 we will discuss later.

Pythagorean musical proportion also produces the ratio of 9:8, which expresses a whole tone. By a similar simple calculation we can deduce the mystical number of 888.

This number had great significance for the ancient Greeks for it was the gematria of the sacred first priest of Apollo, called Olen.

It's worth mentioning here that the founders of early Christianity were well versed in the science and they knew the significance of the number 888 when they created their godman, their first sacred High Priest, Jesus. The name Jesus is a transliteration from the original Aramaic. When it was introduced into the Greek texts, the spelling was adjusted so that the gematria of the name would be 888. Jesus is the 888 of the gospels. He was created along with his name to be the Ogdoad of eights, the powerful triplicity of 8, the number of regeneration and indeed, the number of resurrection.

The harmonic ratios of the musical scale are shown to represent the gods Apollo, Hermes, Zeus, and amongst them Jesus takes his place as the 888.

In his book *Jesus Christ Sun of God*, David Fideler explains this and so much more of the divine symbolism of mathematics in music, that I can only recommend that you go to that source for an incredible in-depth explanation of the subject. We cannot in our quest do anything more, than explain the basics of what gematria is about.

The name of Jesus is an obvious creation. It simply had to add up to 888 so that the rest of the geometric symbolism hidden in the gospel stories would be able to be constructed.

Inventing a name is not surprising, when you consider that the name Abraxas, a Greek solar deity was purposely designed to create the gematria of 365. This is the number of days in the solar year.

The God Mithras, another of the solar gods and a great competitor to the Christian Saviour was also a construct. His name was also designed to display the gematria number of 365.

It was well known to the Church fathers that Jesus had been given a name that was numerically significant. It was our friend Irenaeus who said in his work *Against Heresies,*

"Jesus is a name arithmetically symbolic, consisting of six letters and is known by all those that belong to the called."

Were those "called" the Gnostic Christians, who lived with the philosophy of Pythagoras and his number symbolism?

The number 888 was known as being a symbol of mediation in the theory of music and was also associated with the Spiritual Sun, which Jesus was referred to by Clement of Alexandria. It represented the concept of harmony for gnostic thinkers, and it is in Jesus' manifestation as the Logos that this becomes significant to us.

The Logos was in simple language, the harmony, mediation or "ratio" between God and man, heaven and Earth and it came out of music.

As the 888, Jesus fitted the role perfectly. In effect, He was taking over from the previous incumbent in the job, the great god Apollo.

Apollo demonstrated his credentials for the job by his very name. The Greeks looked at the number 1 as most sacred, the number of the Creator, the Monad, the divine. The number 2 was the number of duality and the first number in the worldly sphere.

From this they created the Pythagorean right-angled triangle with the sides of one unit each, at right angles to each other. By simple geometry and by using Pythagoras' theorem, it is possible to calculate the length of the hypotenuse. It is obviously the square root of 2, which equals 1.414, which is Apollo in his manifestation as the god Pythios.

The square root of 2 was seen as the mediation or harmony between the two sides of the divine 1.

The numbers of 1 related with the square roots of 2 and 3 were highly significant in the sacred symbolic geometry of the Greeks, which was in turn inherited by the Gnostic Christians. So much of the sacred geometry concealed in the New Testament has a basis in the square root of 3 and 2.

The mighty gods of ancient Greece were given names that not only came out of musical harmony but related to each other by the square root of 3 when looked at in their gematria numbers.

Looking again at the mystical number of Jesus, that is 888, we can, if we understand the Greek alphabet, see how much weight it carried when we look at the way the alphabet was depicted.

It was arranged in three rows of eight letters/numbers. The first row is the units, the second is the tens and the third, the hundreds, giving a total of 24 letters or numbers. As the alphabet or number system enclosed everything in creation, 888 was highly symbolic and appears in virtually all of biblical geometry.

Gematria equates phrases and epithets of similar value and gives them extra significance.

You remember the story of Jesus when at the time of baptism, apart from the spooky voice from above, a dove descends from heaven and is made to be quite important in the story, otherwise why mention it?

The gematria of the word "Dove" in original Greek is 801. When Jesus displays himself as everything in creation, he is being portrayed as the Alpha and the Omega, everything between the first and last letters of the Greek alphabet. Jesus is referred to as the Alpha and the Omega in the Book of Revelation (1:8, 21:6, 22:13) and this is symbolic because the gospel writer is telling you that as the Alpha, with a letter value of 1, and as the Omega with a letter value of 800, the total gematria is 801. The dove, in the guise of the heavenly messenger, the Holy Spirit, confirms the all-encompassing spirit that he is to be.

Margaret Starbird, whose work has displayed so much of the lost goddess in Christianity, demonstrates how the number 801 also has connotations with 1080, the feminine number of the moon and as such is able to demonstrate the element of the Sacred Feminine in the gospel stories. The numbers in gematria, such as 801 and 1080 both add up to the mystical 9, which in turn is the triplicity of threes. All have their own profound significance.

The sacred numbers are probably in every book of the Old and New Testaments, and I can say with some confidence that every number mentioned has a deeper meaning, when looked at from a gematria point of view.

When we read a simple phrase or sentence in a gospel story, it can be indicating to the "enlightened" that another message is being conveyed that will enhance the original meaning.

Margaret Starbird and John Michell both indicate examples of this. Starbird points out how the phrase "Lord of the Sabbath" adds up to 888, confirming Him in this role.

She also indicates how the words of the entire verse in Matthew, 1:23 add up to 8880, which is "The Risen Jesus".

These things do not happen by chance. They are words

calculated by their writers to carry the symbolic numbers and enhance our understanding.

You probably ask why it was necessary to do all this complicated stuff in the first place; why bother?

Well, if you remember when we started out on our ever more amazing quest, we discussed the Mystery Religions of the time. We were able to see that the religions were only open to those who were worthy and able to be taught the various levels of understanding until the initiate became one with his god. So it was with early Christianity. Christianity was perceived as a mystery religion and the deeper meanings were taught to the worthy. A simple story on the outside for the simple folk but a spiritual journey on the inner level, for the "seeker of truth". This is why Jesus is made by the gospel writers to sound so complicated when he talks about the Mysteries of the Kingdom and berates the disciples for not understanding what he sees as a simple message.

It is this sort of argument and the use of gematria throughout the New Testament, that confirms my belief in a Gnostic origin for what we read. It was never an historical account; it was a spiritual journey using numbers as a guide.

Another good example of how one piece of gematria can relate to and verify another of a similar value is well displayed by the story and name of John the Baptist.

Elijah the prophet was expected to return to earth and announce the arrival of the superhero Saviour. The people of the day really did expect to see him descend from the heavens, probably in the same flaming chariot that he went up in and confirm to all present that Jesus was the Messiah. This was a big issue with the Jews who could not accept a Christ figure, a Messiah, until that chariot turned up.

They had read in the Old Testament a passage from Malachi 4:1, which read,

For behold, the day cometh that shall burn as an oven and all that do wickedly shall be stubble and the day that cometh shall burn them up, saith the Lord of hosts, that it shall leave them neither root nor branch. And you will trod down the wicked, for they shall be ashes under the soles of your feet. In the day that I shall do this, saith the Lord of hosts, Behold, I will send you Elijah the prophet before the coming of the great and dreadful day of the Lord.

They are still waiting.

The gospel writers knew this was a big problem and that no Jew would listen to a Messiah story without the man in the blazing chariot coming along first. What they did to sort the problem was make Jesus announce that the prophet had already arrived without any mention of chariots. In Matthew 17:10, Jesus tells his apostles,

"In fact, he already has come but he wasn't recognized and was badly mistreated by many. Then the disciples realized he was speaking of John the Baptist."

So, who could argue with that? Well, many probably did and, to a large degree, it is probably a major reason why the Jews rejected Jesus.

But to enhance the words of Jesus, the writer of Revelation includes in chapter 19:10, the telling expression "the testimony of Jesus is the spirit of prophecy."

Gematria comes into play at this point as a backup to the claim made in Matthew 17:10.

What the phrase means is that the truth of the "return" is explained by the "spirit of prophecy".

The gematria of the words "spirit of prophecy" add up to 2220 and, not surprisingly, the gematria of John the Baptist is also 2220.

So, there it is: gematria allows the Baptist to be that necessary "spirit of prophecy". They are both gematria equals of 2220.

So, the gospel writers had no need for a flaming messenger from the skies; they made John the Baptist into a reincarnation of the ever-late Elijah and "proved" it with gematria.

We have discussed how the numbers of musical harmony gave rise to mystical numbers which were revered as holy gematria, such as the 888 of Jesus in the original Greek. Out of the same Pythagorean system came the number 666, probably the best known of the sacred numbers, as far as the public are concerned, and which to most people represents the Beast, the Devil, the Antichrist and Damien.

Well, let's look at it a little closer and finish the chapter with something that will involve the number 666. I guarantee it will amaze you.

The ancient philosophers and mathematicians were fully acquainted with this hugely important number derived from the magic of music and were also aware of its origins from another source. They derived a lot of their mystical number relationships from what they called the Magic Square of the Sun.

This was a square composed of all the numbers between 1 and 36. The numbers are arranged in rows of six in such a way that if you add any line of numbers, horizontally, vertically, or diagonally, the answer is always 111 and of course, the sum total of all the numbers is 666.

If you add any four numbers from a symmetrical position, such as, top left, top right, bottom left and bottom right, or maybe the four numbers in the centre of the square, they will always add up to 74.

This was a very special number for the early Christians who used it to formulate so many of the sacred names, which were the product of this number, at the very foundation of the Magical Square. The number 74 relates many of the names and epithets that we read in the New Testament and they are all related to the number 8880, the raised Jesus.

The number 666 was perceived as a masculine solar number

and as 111 was at its root, this was the triplicity of the monad or the one and was perceived as the spirit of the Sun, not the Sun itself, but its power and its spirit, such was the 666.

If the 666 was allowed to exist without its opposite "feminine" number of 1080, the number relating to the Moon, then the uncontrolled power of the masculine solar 666 would be disastrous and lead to all sorts of breakdown in society.

The harmony of the male and female, the balance of the opposites was essential.

Scholars of gematria when discussing significant numbers which are frequently detected in the Bible, will often quote, 666, 1080, 888, 3168, 1480, 1224, 318, 1925 and several more as very significant recurring numbers. Another number frequently referred to is the number 1746 as the number of fusion.

If you add the two numbers of the Solar and Lunar powers of 666 and 1080, you get the number of fusion, 1746, which is the gematria of very many symbolic phrases and epithets in the gospels. It is obviously an important number to discover.

Again, if you divide 1080 by the 666, you get 1.62 (to two places), which is the highly significant number known as the Golden Mean or Golden Ratio and is present in most ancient architecture and is evident in biology, art, and so much sacred geometry.

John Michell, probably the greatest pioneer of gematria and sacred geometry of contemporary times, points out that the 1746 can be brought out of very many biblical phrases, such as "the universal spirit", "the fruit of the vineyard", " Jerusalem, the city of God", and interestingly, " the grain of mustard seed". This is spoken about in Luke 13:19 and symbolizes the simple seed from which the universal tree developed.

Can this be taken as 1746, the 666 and 1080, being the whole universe?

Mark 4:30 refers to the "grain of mustard seed" as like the Kingdom of God. Again, is he saying that the kingdom of

God is the 1746, the marriage of the masculine with the sacred feminine? The sacred feminine principle, sacred to the Gnostics but abandoned by the Orthodox Church.

When we look at the sacred geometric designs concealed in some of the best-known New Testament stories, it becomes clear how names and phrases have been purposefully created to make the mathematics of the gematria and the subsequent geometry, actually work out.

The sacred geometry can be described as a picture story in numbers, which displays the spiritual, deeper meaning of the myth.

In a very simple, much quoted example, a circle with a circumference of 891 units will have, by calculation, a diameter of 284 units. The number 891 is the gematria of the Greek word Heaven, while 284 is the gematria from the Greek word for God.

God in Heaven is immediately obvious to "those with eyes to see". It's not a trick, it is the only possible diameter for a circle of circumference 891 units. Names were made to fit geometric numbers.

There are two very well-known stories in the New Testament that we must mention in this respect.

The first is the story of the fishes in the net. This is the story of Jesus walking along the water's edge when he sees the disciples fishing. He asks them if they have caught anything, and they tell him that they have caught nothing. Jesus tells them to cast their net on the other side of the boat, which they do. As a result, they haul in a net full of fish. At this point, I would ask you how many fish they caught?

I have asked this question hundreds of times and only once have I received the correct answer.

They hauled in 153 fish as confirmed by John 21:11.

This miraculous story has been shown by John Michell to be a piece of incredible sacred geometry, where all the ingredients of the story and the characters play a role in the gematria that results in the final design, which displays pre-Christian Hellenistic philosophy and the nature of the Logos, understood by the Gnostic Christians.

In a similar way, David Fideler author of *Jesus Christ Sun of God: Ancient Cosmology and early Christian Symbolism*, Quest books, 1993, has been able to "translate" the well-known story of the "Feeding of the Five Thousand", into the highly complicated underlying geometry that it represents.

He shows, quite clearly, how the words in the verses from the New Testament give immediate indications to the basic foundations of the geometry.

Did you ever wonder why it was exactly 5000 people who came to the field where Jesus acted as provider for them?

If you calculate the square root of 5000 you get 70.7, which if you remove the decimal point, is the gematria of the god Hermes. So, we already have reference to the ancient god Hermes in a miraculous story of Jesus.

Fiedler goes on to bring out the geometry, again from the words of the story, which pictorially depict the loaves and fishes by gematria number and demonstrates how the "loaves and fishes" can fulfil the needs of the "five thousand", and of course the sacred 888 makes its appearance in the numbers within the geometry.

Like John Michell, he brings out the philosophy of Greek cosmology within the design and again this was understood by the early Gnostic Christians.

These stories are both older than Christianity itself and were both used and adapted by the Gnostic followers of the Christ myth to convey their message of Jesus. The fishes in the net story is recorded in the life story of Pythagoras and it was probably he that created it and this was hundreds of years before the advent of the Christians.

I asked you how many fish were in the net and the answer was 153. This is no arbitrary number chosen at random. It is one of the most sacred numbers which comes out of biblical geometry and is used by Christians to represent many sacred elements of their faith, even if they are not aware of it.

Both of the miraculous stories that tell of Greek cosmology and the nature of the Logos involve geometry that involves the intersection of circles, which produces the shape of a fish.

This fish shape, called the *Vesica piscis*, has a constant ratio of length to width, regardless of the size of the similar circles that intersect it.

This ratio is 265:153 and was known to the ancient geometers as the number of the fish, it is also the fraction that depicts the square root of 3.

The almond shape thus created was known by many sacred names and because of its womb shape, became associated with the sacred feminine.

The figure of Jesus in many works of art, cathedrals and churches is frequently depicted set inside this shape. We should note that as the Messiah of the new age of Pisces, it is no coincidence that we are finding a lot of fish symbolism in the gospels.

It was a vital part of the geometry and Margaret Starbird should be congratulated for recognizing that Mary Magdalene when known by her epithet, "the Magdalene", has the gematria of 153. This is not a coincidence. She really was the Sacred Feminine.

The number 153 had enormous importance to the Gnostic Christians, but probably very few understand that in the Church today. Most think it is a simple representation of the Christian idea of Jesus and the disciples as the "fishers of men" (Mark 1:17). Probably only a handful of apologists who refuse to step outside of the confines of the New Testament, and that includes most of the Church's leaders, will be aware of the sacred mathematics that created it and the story, too, that it comes out of.

The almond shape, the shape of the fish and the incredible inherent geometry and symbolism within it, is evident, too, in the shapes of the arches in our huge cathedrals, and of course in our ordinary churches. Why is the mitre of the Bishop of Rome so obviously a fish shape? You will see the same shape depicted in stained glass windows and in its simplest form, on the back of motor cars as a symbol of Christianity.

When they moved into the great age of Pisces, they really let the faithful know about it.

Let me make an observation that should be remembered and thought about very deeply.

None of this highly complicated mathematical, geometric harmony would be possible if all the names of the active participants had not been intentionally crafted by the brilliant early Pythagorean scholars who created it, and the gospel writers who played their part in the spiritual symbolism.

The names of Jesus Christ, Simon Peter, Apollo, Hermes and others were constructs, taken from numbers of music and geometric harmony. They were based on square roots, multiples, and all came together in the "sacred harmony", to display the nature of the Hellenistic concept and how it was accepted by the Christians as the inheritors of the New Age.

Ask yourself, if the names are inventions to convey a spiritual message, is it possible that the participants are inventions too? Nobody believes that Apollo, Zeus, Pythios or Hermes ever walked the earth but their partners in the very same geometry, as it exists in the New Testament, are still considered as historical characters!

We did say earlier that we would conclude our look at gematria with a bit more information about the number 666.

If you read chapter 13:11 in the Book of Revelation, it describes the now infamous "Beast", the dark Satanic character who was the Antichrist.

As a result, that number 666 has had nothing but sinister

connotations associated with it.

The chapter reads "Here is wisdom, let him that hath understanding count the number of the beast, for it is the number of a man: and his number is six hundred, threescore and six."

For centuries people have suggested a variety of names and even empires that they perceived as having the gematria of 666. Some were quite bizarre and some sounded quite possible.

It has been generally accepted by most theologians and probably most Orthodox Christians, that it refers to the Emperor Nero, who, it is true, can be perceived as having the 666 gematria if you include his title of Caesar.

It was easy to accept this because like Pope Leo X, nobody had a good word to say about Nero. It would sound like common sense for the early Christians to see him as the Antichrist and as such he fitted the 666 bill perfectly. And so, it was, for a long time, Nero has been the embodiment of the 666, the Beast of the Book of Revelation.

Scholars of gematria were never too happy about this. There was something not quite right.

For a few years I was convinced that there was more to this story and the clue was in the wording that was not as straightforward as it seemed to be.

I could not understand why the Gnostic writer who put this together was asking me to count the number of the Beast and then gave it to me quite freely as 666?

This had me beaten and I tried a variety of gematria possibilities and juggled with words and phrases in the text. Nothing came out of it.

When I discovered the work of John Michell everything became clear and the whole thing fitted into place.

There is no doubt that John Michell as one of the modern pioneers of Gematria and sacred number, will one day be seen as the genius that he was.

In his book *The Dimensions of Paradise: The Proportions and Symbolic Numbers of Ancient Cosmology*, Adventures Unlimited Press, 2008, he explains how he, too, was aware of the fact that the number 666 was readily given, meaning that another number was hidden in the text.

He took the words from the final part of the text: "and his number is six hundred, threescore and six" and converted them from their Greek original into the gematria of the whole phrase, which came to the unbelievable number of 2368.

2368 is the gematria of the full title of Jesus Christ.

To understand this, you must abandon the idea that has grown up around the 666 number and think back to what you have learnt so far in our spiritual journey.

At the beginning of this book, I described the nature of those early Christians known to us as the Gnostics. We saw how their concept of the Jesus figure differed widely from that of the developing orthodox Church, with its bishops and priests; something the Gnostics did not agree with. You will remember that these Christians did not see the figure of Jesus as a living, flesh and blood, historical character. For them he was a spirit and nothing else.

You will also remember what we said about the inherent character of that number 666. It was meant to represent the unbalanced power of the solar principle and if unbalanced, would lead to tyranny and chaos.

What the writer of revelation was saying, as understood by John Michell and the thinking of the Gnostics, is that the figure of the dying man on the cross being worshipped by the Church, was something they could not agree with. For them, he was never human and only God should be worshipped and revered. This worship of a human Jesus would lead to the negative manifestations of the number 666. The image and worship of the man on the cross would lead to all the things that the unbalanced 666 would inflict.

From what you know, from our study so far, you will be able to see the probability of this explanation.

Those who argue against this extraction of the 2368 by John Michell, usually know nothing at all about gematria, or Gnosticism in the early years of Christianity.

Chapter 14

Reviewing all the Evidence

If this was a book written by an orthodox Christian apologist defending the veracity of the gospels, Acts and the Letters of Paul, then I imagine whatever had been put forward for their case would prove that the Bible, in its totality, is indeed, the inerrant word of God and as such, is perfect and contains no historical inaccuracies.

Having examined so much detail about the very many aspects of history that must be understood before even starting on an analysis of biblical texts, I think that you, the reader, will agree with me that the gospels are a thousand times more complicated than what you thought before we started out.

Do you still think that nothing we have uncovered has made any real impression on a literal interpretation of the New Testament, and the story of the godman travelling around Palestine doing good deeds, dying a cruel death, and then coming back again as flesh and blood, really is exactly how the Bible described it?

I regularly meet with literal believers of the Bible who simply do not have the capacity within themselves to examine the arguments against the historical nature of the story, or even listen to the arguments in the first place. I am regularly shouted down by those who have never looked at the history of the times from outside the pages of the Bible and use ignorance and often abuse, as their only weapon.

Their total lack of knowledge of the elements we have examined in some depth means, quite simply, that they do not exist.

It is as though they are saying to me, "if I don't know it, it doesn't exist."

Never was this point more evident than the dozens of times I have tried to explain the concept of gematria and its use by the early Christians. The subject is met with blank stares and a belief that it is some sort of code put together by Nostradamus, able to predict global disasters and even lottery winners.

At the very outset, we saw how there were early philosophers who maintained an ancient way of spiritual thinking and were known to us as the Gnostics.

Their profound Pythagorean and Platonic thinking was the basis for the way they perceived the character as Jesus. He was, for them, a spirit and nothing else. He was sent by the true God in the Pleroma to guide them to the divine within themselves and the myth they created around this Saviour was never meant to be taken literally. This is a major consideration in our search for the fundamental basis of the cult's origins.

But who was this Jesus character and where did he come from?

This is the part of the enquiry that leaves too many unexplained problems. It has always been a major issue with so many theologians that St Paul never relates to a living Jesus. He evangelizes only about the Christ, not the man but the coming Messiah.

He has no apparent knowledge of the life of Jesus and never mentions any miracles, good deeds or the essential virgin birth. It is as though he knew nothing about these events and I do not think he did.

The gospels were still not written, and the supposed history of the man had yet to be created. We must add this to the mix and not lose sight of the wood for the trees. It's another major consideration.

Paul had a dream or a vision about a pre-existent saviour figure, one the mystical Essenes or Therapeutae had been expecting for a hundred years and more before Paul's vision, and he brought it to fruition.

I am convinced that Paul was a Gnostic. Without knowing how the Gnostics worshipped their God and the philosophy they lived by, Paul could easily escape the accusation of being called a Gnostic. He used the language of the Gnostics and he openly accepts that the resurrection is not "flesh and blood". He talks continually about a mystical Christ, as one in heaven with the Father. Most tellingly, he does not give us any indication of a time or a place for the events he relates to.

This is important, because I suspect with good evidence that Paul is looking back more than a hundred years, and is bringing to life the saviour of the Essenes, or is it the long-awaited Joshua figure from centuries before?

Why does Paul not tell us what stories the main Apostles, Peter and James, were able to relate when he met them? Again, not a word about the good deeds or miracles.

Without repeating what we have already discussed about Paul and the Church of God, there is just too much left unanswered to give any credibility to a living Jesus, the man that he was aware of. Christian scholars try endlessly to complicate the Pauline accounts by looking for elements of the story that simply do not seem to exist. Maybe the story was written by Paul and was not meant to be, from the outset, as simple as it appears? He was only telling us the essentials that he was able to.

I have discussed this with gospel scholars who use the Book of Acts to embellish the stories of Paul and who will readily delve deep into Luke and bring out extractions that I am not convinced are there.

If Paul knew about it, he would have spread the gospel far and wide.

It does not seem reasonable to use the Book of Acts to tell us things about Paul when he does not seem to be aware of them himself.

Not only is Paul apparently unaware of a Jesus life story but other scriptural texts from the time show a similar lack of interest in the miraculous story.

The politics of the time required the Church and probably Bishop Ignatius to organise a potted history of the miracle worker to give some substance to the developing story as it stood. The Gnostics were winning the battle with their spiritual, non-human Christ, but that changed when the populace was given access to a life story that they could relate to.

Let us not forget what we learnt about the very many competing religions, so similar in so many ways. The Hellenistic philosophy had permeated the religion of the early Christians just as it was demonstrated in those other mystery religions.

We simply cannot ignore the influence of the Solar deities and the astrotheology that came out of it; Christianity was immersed in it.

We really must make a big mental note, in our considerations, that we cannot allow the fact that there are no reliable attestations to the living Jesus, from any historian at the time, to go unnoticed.

This is a huge problem for the defenders of the literal truth theory and yet, nobody has been able to demonstrate any reliable reference from outside the Bible to a man who was supposedly the most famous man that ever lived.

Throughout my studies of this intriguing and important subject, the one aspect that I think will eventually revolutionize the whole concept of Christianity and its belief systems, is the growing awareness of Gematria and Sacred Geometry, crafted by geniuses into the words of the supposedly historical accounts of the Jesus figure, as he performed wondrous deeds.

We have seen how the story of Jesus and the 153 fishes in the net was a story created by Pythagoras and is told about him in the works we still have about his life story. It was old when the Bible writers used it to enhance the hidden truths about their hero.

It was not a real story. It did not happen, but people will still read this with a sense of awe, unaware of the complicated maths and geometry going on in the myth.

I will confidently predict that within the next twenty years this subject of Gematria will become much more widely known and when, as we said, some people of influence latch onto it, the ball will start rolling and it will not stop.

It is a hugely important aspect of our investigation and yet, I have not met a single member of the clergy who has any understanding of it at all or even that it exists, nor are they prepared to admit to it.

There is no intention within the pages of this small book to be in any way offensive to the people who still perceive the Jesus story as exactly as it is written and firmly believe that it was never influenced by other cults, or indeed, never changed by the scribes since it was set down two thousand years ago.

I would simply ask you to look at the story from a broader perspective and if nothing else, be aware that there really is another world outside the scope of the very limited confines of a literal reading of the New Testament.

A Final Word

Based on the evidence, I see the Christian story as having developed from a Gnostic beginning. A vision perceived by St Paul, of a long dead, pre-existent Saviour figure.

Paul brought him to life: the Essenes originally, and ultimately the Gnostic Christians of the diaspora, viewed him as a divine teacher who taught them the meaning of the divine and the journey within themselves, to become as one with that Divine Spirit. And it was the Gnostic Christians in the diaspora that accepted Paul's version of the Messianic messenger. For them, he was the Messiah but only in spirit. Christianity grew not in the biblical Holy Land but in the learning centres of the Greek diaspora, where the melting pot of cultures made its mark.

As time went on, the fledgling Church realized they needed more than a spirit to expand their growing power. The bishops needed an historical man, so they created one.

All the elements of what was common in the day were used in the creation of a superhero, who the Gnostics knew had never existed and certainly did not wish to worship as a man on a cross.

The net result was a man who was a Christ and who fulfilled all the necessary requirements for the Church and followers alike. He fulfilled the credentials required by the Old Testament and in a very clever way, he became all things to all men, depending on how you wanted to perceive the myth. His real origins were lost to history, but it was the clever gospel writers who included the hidden truths about the "mysteries" that Jesus is made to allude to in the myths created on his behalf.

The language of Gematria cannot be denied and it is telling us that Jesus as the 888 is a Gnostic myth with a deeply spiritual significance and it is for you, the "initiate of the mysteries", to find that divine within yourself!

Key Historical Figures

Alexander the Great circa 355–323 BCE: Army general from Macedonia. Took over the empires of Persia and Egypt and launched the Hellenistic empire.

Apollonius of Tyana: Miracle worker who travelled around the Empire in the first century CE. Considered to have been a Pythagorean philosopher with a life story very similar to Jesus.

Carpocrates: Early second-century Gnostic who developed a controversial school of gnostic belief. Thought to have had associations with the Secret Gospel of Mark.

Celsus: A thorn in the side of Christian Fathers in the late second century CE. Much of what we know of him comes from the work of Origen. Considered the cult of emerging Christianity to be nothing more than a copy of what already existed in the religions of his day.

Clement of Alexandria 150–216 CE: Early Church father considered by many as a gnostic. Student of the Greek philosophers and called the new faith of Christianity the "New Song".

Euripides 484–405 BCE: Author of the mystery play *The Bacchae*.

Eusebius 260–340 CE: Became the official historian to the Emperor Constantine and was considered totally unreliable in his approach to accurate detail. Some scholars think he was responsible for interpolations into earlier histories to give it more credibility.

Herodotus 484–425 BCE: Ancient Greek historian. Travelled widely and wrote about the mysteries of Osiris.

Hierocles circa 303 CE: Historian who accused Christians of plagiarism when they created their Jesus figure as a direct copy of Apollonius of Tyana. His works were refuted by Eusebius.

Hippolytus of Rome 170–236 CE: Author of *Refutation of All Heresies*. Considered all Gnostics to be heretics. His works criticizing the Gnostics have provided much information about their beliefs.

Irenaeus 130–202 CE: Arch opponent of the Gnostics and his work *Against Heresies*, gives much information about their beliefs. Became Bishop of Lyons in 178 CE. A tireless defender of the orthodox faith.

Jerome 340–420 CE: Defender of the orthodox faith. Translated the Bible into Latin.

Josephus 38–107 CE: Romano Jewish historian whose works *The Jewish War* and *Antiquities of the Jews* tell us much about first-century Judaism.

Justin Martyr 100–165 CE: Refuted the works and beliefs of the gnostic sects. Wrote in defence of early orthodoxy.

Marcion: Leader of Gnostic school around 144 CE. Considered the God of the Old Testament as a false god and looked upon Paul as the "Great Apostle".

Origen 185–255 CE: Alexandrian teacher and scholar with profound interest in Platonic theory. Some of his works are distinctly gnostic although he was considered a literalist.

Philo: Philo Judaeus circa 30 BCE–45 CE. Jewish theologian with deep interest in Platonic and Pythagorean philosophy. Recorded much history from his time including information about the Essenes and Therapeutae. Makes no mention of Jesus at all, although he lived during the period that Jesus was supposed to have been in the Holy Land.

Philostratus the Elder 170–247 CE: Biographer of Apollonius of Tyana. Tells the amazingly similar life story to that of Jesus.

Plato 429–348 BCE: Studied the teachings of Pythagoras. One of the most influential and learned philosophers of his time. Profound interest in the Orphic mysteries.

Pliny: Pliny the Elder 23–79 CE: Influential author, philosopher and army commander of the Roman Empire. Makes no reference to Jesus Christ in his works.

Plutarch 46–124 CE: Priest and philosopher. Great supporter of Platonic philosophy.

Porphyry 233–305 CE: Neo Platonic philosopher who authored a polemic against the early Christians, *Adversus Christianos*.

Pythagoras circa 570–496 BCE: Greek cosmologist, philosopher, mathematician and follower of the Orphic mysteries. Believed that number was the root of everything and had a huge influence on the works of Plato.

Simon Magus: Founder of the Simonian Gnostic sect circa 35 CE: Little known about him except what we read from his detractors. Described variously as a Jew, a Christian, a magician, a sorcerer, a pseudo-Messiah and an arch-heretic.

Socrates circa 469–399 BCE: One of the best-known Greek philosophers of antiquity. Credited as one of the founders of Western philosophy.

Tacitus 56–117 CE: Roman historian and author of the *Annals*.

Tertullian 160–220 CE: Early Church father. Fought endlessly against the heretics but was a pagan until his middle years.

Valentinus 100–180 CE: Most famous of the Alexandrian gnostic teachers. Thought to have authored the gnostic Gospel of Truth. Founded a Gnostic school in Rome.

THE NEW OPEN SPACES

Throughout the two thousand years of Christian tradition there have been, and still are, groups and individuals that exist in the margins and upon the edge of faith. But in Christianity's contrapuntal history it has often been these outcasts and pioneers that have forged contemporary orthodoxy out of former radicalism as belief evolves to engage with and encompass the ever-changing social and scientific realities. Real faith lies not in the comfortable certainties of the Orthodox, but somewhere in a half-glimpsed hinterland on the dirt track to Emmaus, where the Death of God meets the Resurrection, where the supernatural Christ meets the historical Jesus, and where the revolution liberates both the oppressed and the oppressors.
Welcome to Christian Alternative... a space at the edge where the light shines through.
If you have enjoyed this book, why not tell other readers by posting a review on your preferred book site.

Recent bestsellers from Christian Alternative are:

Bread Not Stones
The Autobiography of An Eventful Life
Una Kroll
The spiritual autobiography of a truly remarkable woman
and a history of the struggle for ordination in the Church of
England.
Paperback: 978-1-78279-804-0 ebook: 978-1-78279-805-7

The Quaker Way
A Rediscovery
Rex Ambler
Although fairly well known, Quakerism is not well understood.
The purpose of this book is to explain how Quakerism works as
a spiritual practice.
Paperback: 978-1-78099-657-8 ebook: 978-1-78099-658-5

Blue Sky God
The Evolution of Science and Christianity
Don MacGregor
Quantum consciousness, morphic fields and blue-sky
thinking about God and Jesus the Christ.
Paperback: 978-1-84694-937-1 ebook: 978-1-84694-938-8

Celtic Wheel of the Year
Tess Ward
An original and inspiring selection of prayers combining
Christian and Celtic Pagan traditions, and interweaving their
calendars into a single pattern of prayer for every morning
and night of the year.
Paperback: 978-1-90504-795-6

Christian Atheist
Belonging without Believing
Brian Mountford
Christian Atheists don't believe in God but miss him: especially the transcendent beauty of his music, language, ethics, and community.
Paperback: 978-1-84694-439-0 ebook: 978-1-84694-929-6

Compassion Or Apocalypse?
A Comprehensible Guide to the Thoughts of René Girard
James Warren
How René Girard changes the way we think about God and the Bible, and its relevance for our apocalypse-threatened world.
Paperback: 978-1-78279-073-0 ebook: 978-1-78279-072-3

Diary Of A Gay Priest
The Tightrope Walker
Rev. Dr. Malcolm Johnson
Full of anecdotes and amusing stories, but the Church is still a dangerous place for a gay priest.
Paperback: 978-1-78279-002-0 ebook: 978-1-78099-999-9

Do You Need God?
Exploring Different Paths to Spirituality Even For Atheists
Rory J.Q. Barnes
An unbiased guide to the building blocks of spiritual belief.
Paperback: 978-1-78279-380-9 ebook: 978-1-78279-379-3

Readers of ebooks can buy or view any of these bestsellers by clicking on the live link in the title. Most titles are published in paperback and as an ebook. Paperbacks are available in traditional bookshops. Both print and ebook formats are available online.

Find more titles and sign up to our readers' newsletter at
http://www.johnhuntpublishing.com/christianity
Follow us on Facebook at
https://www.facebook.com/ChristianAlternative